# Haunted Rhode Island

## Thomas D'Agostino

### Photography by Arlene Nicholson

Schiffer Publishing Ltd

4880 Lower Valley Road, Atglen, PA 19310 USA

# Dedication

This book is dedicated to my wife, Arlene, who has always believed in me.

Copyright © 2006 by Thomas D'Agostino
Library of Congress Control Number: 2005931924

All rights reserved. No part of this work may be reproduced or used in any form or by any means—graphic, electronic, or mechanical, including photocopying or information storage and retrieval systems—without written permission from the publisher.

The scanning, uploading and distribution of this book or any part thereof via the Internet or via any other means without the permission of the publisher is illegal and punishable by law. Please purchase only authorized editions and do not participate in or encourage the electronic piracy of copyrighted materials.

"Schiffer," "Schiffer Publishing Ltd. & Design," and the "Design of pen and ink well" are registered trademarks of Schiffer Publishing Ltd.

Designed by Joseph M. Riggio Jr.
Type set in Zapf Chancery Bd BT/Humanist521 BT

ISBN: 0-7643-2350-4
Printed in China

Published by Schiffer Publishing Ltd.
4880 Lower Valley Road
Atglen, PA 19310
Phone: (610) 593-1777; Fax: (610) 593-2002
E-mail: Info@schifferbooks.com

For the largest selection of fine reference books on this and related subjects, please visit our web site at
**www.schifferbooks.com**
We are always looking for people to write books on new and related subjects. If you have an idea for a book please contact us at the above address.

This book may be purchased from the publisher.
Include $3.95 for shipping.
Please try your bookstore first.
You may write for a free catalog.

In Europe, Schiffer books are distributed by
Bushwood Books
6 Marksbury Ave.
Kew Gardens
Surrey TW9 4JF England
Phone: 44 (0) 20 8392-8585; Fax: 44 (0) 20 8392-9876
E-mail: info@bushwoodbooks.co.uk
Free postage in the U.K., Europe; air mail at cost.

# Contents

# Acknowledgments

I would like to thank my wife, Arlene, who took all the photographs for this book and never turned down an opportunity to visit or investigate a haunted location. Special thanks to those who shared their time and experiences with me for this book. They include Domenic Iocone, Eva-Marie Belheumer, and all the other great people of the Stagecoach Tavern, Randy Fabricant of the Agincourt Inn, Mary Rolando of the Black Duck Inn, Louis Seymour and Patrick Grimes from the Beechwood Theatre Company in Newport, Shadowlands.com, Rhode Island Paranormal, Tri-State Paranormal Research Group, Carl and Keith Johnson who are a wealth of information on everything, Christopher Martin and Dan Hillman at Quahog.com. (If it is about Rhode Island they can help), Glenn Hopkins, everyone at the Rhode Island Historical Society, Dick Martin of the Observer Publications, Susan Smitten, *FATE* magazine, Seth Bromley of the *Neighbors* newspaper, all the people at *What's News* from Rhode Island College, and Virginia Goncalo and her class at William J. Johnson Middle School in Colchester, Connecticut. I must also give great mention to Sheila Williams, Rocco and Gail Desimone, Robert Vespia, John Boitano, Dennis Mann, Kevin Fay, Chris Moreau, and my brothers and sisters for their help during the many places we traveled to in writing this book. Last, but certainly not least, I would like to thank all the people who wanted to remain nameless for fear of being scoffed at about their experiences. I am certain this book will prove to them that they are in very good company.

# Introduction

Rhode Island has always been known as the Ocean State. That is because it has more coastline per landmass than any other state in the Union. This fact overshadows the inland mysteries that have made this one of the most notorious states for the strange and terrifying in the whole country.

I must confess, when researching for this book, I had no idea that such a small state could yield such a large population of ghosts, vampires, folklore, and other eerie tales of history.

A ten-minute drive from the bustling capital city of Providence transports you back one hundred years in time. You are now gazing upon endless stone walls and fields where animals lay and graze. Old barns and farmhouses dot the wooded scenery. Also lurking in the shadows of these parcels of land are countless phantoms, legends of vampires, witches, and other historical haunted wonders that rival, if not surpass, territories many times their size.

Rhode Island is only forty-eight miles long by thirty-seven miles wide. It is one of the original thirteen colonies. In fact it was the last to join, under duress, threatened with being shut off from future aid from the other colonies during enemy attacks to come. Yes, the stubborn Yankee disposition of today's ghosts was in their hearts and souls when they walked the earth as living entities. In 1635, Reverend William Blackstone from Boston was the first white man to settle in what is now Rhode Island. Roger Williams and his band of religious outcasts formed a colony in Providence a year later. That was when the state was recognized as officially settled. It is safe to say that many a tale or event can be nurtured over this amount of time.

The following pages contain some of the most amazing stories history can tell, from rural Rhode Island, where fearful families dug up the dead in search of vampires, to Indian ghosts searching for justice and revenge. You will encounter haunted lighthouses and public houses, ghost dogs, phantom automobiles, and even haunted trees. There are many different kinds of spooky entities roving the Ocean State.

A tourist of the paranormal can visit almost every site in this book on a single weekend. Some places in this writing may require permission to visit or have a tour fee. It is a small price to pay for the chance of an encounter with the "other side."

So, grab this book, a map, and hit the ghostly trail. If you get lost and see an old man carrying a broken shovel in Moosup Valley, or a grayish dog in the road near Wallum Lake, or even an Indian woman searching the side of the woods near Tarkiln, you will know you have found your way.

# Barrington

## Saint Andrews School—
## The Headmaster has Never Left
## the Building

Several years ago I was working on a project at Saint Andrews School when a strange incident occurred. At the time I was working in a room just off of the gym. There was a piano on the other side of the gym in the corner, so I assumed it was also used as an auditorium as well. I was on the other side of a doorway leading to the large room when I heard the piano play. It sounded for several notes then stopped. I looked around the doorway but the room was empty. At first I thought it was a joke and resumed my duties. I figured it was one of the people I had gotten to know during my work there.

I rolled this around in my mind, thinking to myself that they might get frustrated due to my lack of interest in their prank. Then it happened again. Four or five notes emanated from the instrument. This time I quickly whirled around the door as the last note echoed into space. There was no one at the piano. There was no way anyone could have gotten out of the room so fast because the door was at least thirty feet from the instrument. Even if they were Olympic runners, I still would have heard the flight of their footsteps echoing off the high ceiling from the hardwood floor.

I approached the piano, expecting someone to jump out of some hidden door or covering of which I was not aware. I figured now they could have their delight and scare me. I would even pretend to be startled by the folly. When I got to the piano and checked out the area, I realized I had been alone in the room the whole time. I was now truly startled. I felt like it was time to leave the room and did so.

While meandering down the hall, I saw the usual afternoon maintenance crew I had befriended and made a comment on how the place is haunted. He asked what happened and I told him, though somewhat reluctantly, about the piano. I also told him I had experienced other paranormal phenomena before, so it was not new to me, only disturbing at the moment. This is when he divulged a secret to me. The place *is* haunted. Of the various buildings on the campus, the one we were in has been haunted forever. He spoke of how he has seen shadows in the hallway at night. He also mentioned I was not the first to hear the ghostly music coming from the old piano. It is a room he always cleaned while people were still in the building, then secured tight for the night. "Ghost or not, that place gives me the creeps when I am alone in here," he confided to me. I certainly could not blame him.

Another building in particular, The McVickar building, seems to command the most otherworldly attention from the living. It is the first edifice you see as you pull into the educational facility.

Saint Andrews School was founded in 1893 by Reverend William Merrick Chapin, who was at the time rector of Saint Johns Episcopal Church in Barrington. It was originally a school for homeless boys. Legend

The McVickar building at St. Andrews, said to be haunted by a former schoolmaster.

has it that he started the facility after taking in a homeless youth begging on the streets. By 1896 it was a self-sustaining community consisting of an orphanage, social service facility, school, and farm where the boys and teachers worked together to grow their own food.

As Headmaster, Reverend Chapin was a just and giving soul who oversaw the daily activity of the complex. When he passed on, the responsibility of Headmaster was passed on in hopes of maintaining the dream the reverend had seen come to fruitation. Others however could not rise to the level of greatness the Reverend Chapin had achieved and by the 1960s the farming had discontinued and the facility became strictly academic in nature. Coed classes began in 1981. This must have caused much dismay to the spirit of Pastor Chapin, as he now haunts the very grounds he loved and nurtured in life.

The McVickar building is his building of choice. His apparition is seen in a red cape wandering the halls at all hours. Students and teachers can attest to his specter sauntering down the corridors of the old building. The maintenance crew experienced his presence quite often in the old building. You will feel a cold breeze overtake you and sense his unearthly presence just before he appears. While sweeping the floor one night before closing, a maintenance worker noticed the shadow of a man drift across the hall out of the corner of his eye. He told me that when he looked up he saw the person in a cape or shroud standing down the hall looking at him before disappearing into thin air. After that he never went in the building alone again at night. Whether or not it is the old headmaster also playing the piano is a mystery as no one has ever seen the invisible musician. They have only heard the few notes of a melody that is of another world.

Saint Andrews School is located at 63 Federal Road. Take Interstate Route 195 to Route 114 (Wampanoag Trail South) to Route 103 South. Take a right onto Federal Road.

# Bristol
## Colt-Andrews School

The children of this elementary school have to share their classrooms with some rather unusual guests. This particular school is haunted by the Colt and Andrews families, whose portraits hang in the auditorium. Strange voices and smells permeate the boy's bathroom. This creates quite a fright in the children who unexpectedly hear the ethereal voices out of nowhere. Members of the maintenance crew claim to have seen specters in the halls at night after the school was locked up as well as teachers who dare stay beyond the normal school hours. They immediately recognize the wispy faces as those of the two families who graciously donated the buildings. It could be that they are staying after to make sure the dowries are well used. The Colt building was erected out of marble and bronze in 1906 by Samuel Pomeroy Colt for the town. The Andrews school was built in 1938 from money left to the town by Robert D. Andrews in memory of his father, Robert Shaw Andrews.

They now serve as elementary classrooms where students of the fourth and fifth grades travel back and forth between the buildings. The Colt section has five classrooms, auditorium, music room, art room, and cafeteria. Andrews has seven classrooms, a gym, library, and media center.

The complex is located at 570 Hope Street. Take Interstate Route 195 to Route 36. Take a right onto Route 114 to the center of Warren. Bear left onto Route 114 towards Bristol. The school is on the left.

## Colt State Park

Colt State Park is known as the gem of Rhode Island parks. It was once a vast farm owned by Samuel Pomeroy Colt, who was born on January 10, 1853. His father was the brother of Samuel Colt, who was the maker of the revolver that won the West.

Samuel Pomeroy Colt founded the Industrial Trust Company Bank in 1887 and later went on to be chairman of the board of the United States Rubber Company. His wealth enabled him to buy three adjacent farms overlooking the Narragansett Bay and combine them with a system of roads. These are the trails and roads that make up the park's scenic walkways and bike paths today. Buster Crabbe, a famous movie actor of *Tarzan* fame, once played on the farm, as his father was the first superintendent of the land.

Samuel Colt died on August 13, 1921, from a stroke and the land stayed in the family as per his will until August 3, 1965, when the state purchased it for public use. The great barn that housed Colt's prize-winning herd is now the park office. A stable hand is said to have died in that barn and now stays behind, turning on lights that the staff is sure they shut off. He also opens doors that were supposedly locked by staff members upon leaving the building. Many staff members have secured the building for a few minutes to check on the park. They have come back to the office a few moments later to find the doors completely open with no foul play or damage to the building.

Interim park manager, Walter Rocha, claims he has seen nothing unusual in his short stay there, but other workers claimed to have seen the frightening ghosts of two little girls walking along the path near the beach. They vanished into thin air each time they were approached. The eerie sound of little girls giggling is also heard permeating the woods nearby. Park workers are not the only living people to see this unnerving sight. Tourists shaken with fear have reported to many a park ranger of their encounter with the ghostly children. It is known that two little girls drowned off the point near the beach in the 1970s. Take a tour or a swim at the point. Who knows what you will bump into on a grassy path overlooking the still but not silent Colt State Park.

Admission is free and the park is open from sunrise to sunset. There are other buildings on the property worth checking out for possible ghostly activity. To get there, take Interstate Route 195 East to Exit 7, Route 114. Follow Route 114 to Hope Street.

# Roger Williams University Theater

Known to students and faculty as the "Barn" because it was originally two nineteenth century barns that were brought to the site and made into one large building. The theater is home to a ghost the students have dubbed "Banquo." It is likely to be the spirit of a farmhand who froze to death many years ago in the hayloft of one of the barns. It is said that he fell asleep up there after a long night of drinking with other friends. He was either too embarrassed at his condition to show himself to his employer or he was just too intoxicated to make the trip to his own bed. No one knows for sure. They only know he has never left the last place he saw in life.

He now makes his presence known to theater patrons by moving the heavy black curtains during rehearsals and shows. People will see one curtain move, then maybe the other or they will both ripple as if someone was making their entrance onto the stage. Many people in the theater have heard strange names being called out from nowhere only to find there is no source for the voice. They then realize it is Banquo looking for attention as the voice reverberates through the high ceilings and then into oblivion. He is also known for very significant and sudden cold spots that move about the building in a most human fashion. Sometimes they even follow a person as they move around in the theater.

The University is located at 1 Old Ferry Road off Route 114 in the southern tip of Bristol. It is a large yellow building visible as soon as you enter the university. The theater phone number is (401) 254-3666.

Roger Williams University Theater, where the ghost named "Banquo" roams.

A view of the "Barn" as seen from Route 114.

# Arnolds Point Fort

Arnolds Point is one of the many aban-doned military forts in Rhode Island. The Ocean State as we know it was a major stra-tegic naval point during Word War II and vari-ous forts were erected to protect the coast-line and naval base at Quonset Point. Though many of the soldiers stationed at the forts never saw military action, they still seem to linger on long after the fort has decayed and crumbled.

It is now reported haunted by those who served in the fort's heyday from World War II until its closing shortly after the war. The voices of the defenders of freedom can be heard shouting through the thin veil of time and wraiths in uniform have been seen along the edge of the old garrison. The fort is on Lehigh Hill west of Route 114 and south of Willow Lane about 1 mile south of the Bristol Ferry. Take Interstate Route 195 to Route 114 South.

# Bristol Ferry

An old "D" class landing still harbors a few people and many stories of ghosts along the docks. A few "old timers" claim the sailors of yesteryear still walk the old docks, maybe searching for their comrades or ships. Not much more information on this area is available, except it is also labeled as a ghost town on various websites.

It is located west of the Mount Hope Bridge on Route 114 just south of Bristol.

# Bristol Ferry Fort

This is another abandoned Navy fort. There is no definitive information on who haunts it, but the "locals" say it is haunted. It might be worth checking out. I am including it in this chapter because it is a reported site of activity; whether it is true or not, you can judge for yourself.

The fort sits due east of the Mount Hope Bridge, south of Bristol. The Mount Hope Bridge connects Bristol with Portsmouth, Middletown, and Newport. Follow the directions for the previous sites.

# Burrillville
## Round Top Road

A farmhouse built in the 1730s by the Richardson family is reported to harbor some evil spirits. The building has been plagued through the years with violent deaths and suicides. A beggar was given refuge from the cold but froze to death in the shed and another man met the same fate when, for some reason, he fell asleep in front of the house on his wagon.

Former owners have seen an old woman in a gray dress with her head hanging to one side shrieking "GET OUT, GET OUT, OR I WILL DRIVE YOU OUT WITH DEATH AND GLOOM!!!"

A clothes hanger flew out of the closet and whacked an owner, Mrs. Perron, in the head several times and an orange taken from the refrigerator bled when cut open.

Round Top Road is off of Route 98 in the Harrisville section of town. The owners respect their privacy therefore no further information can be given.

## Buck Hill Road

The wraith of a dog appears and disappears in the vicinity of Buck Hill. The animal is grayish-white and is often seen lying in the road. When one gets out of the car to check on the spectral creature, it vanishes right in front of the concerned motorist. Some people have reported seeing the dog appear in their headlights snarling and showing glowing teeth at the car. As they hit the brakes to avoid hitting the animal, the dog vanishes in front of them. Some get out of the car and look around for the dog they thought they just hit. Others know better.

Residents of the area have witnessed the phantom creature many times but no one knows why it haunts the vicinity or where it came from. Popular belief is that is was once someone's pet who was hit by a car long before the neighborhood was built up. Unlike the evil black dogs of Great Britain, this wraith reportedly poses no deathly harm to its witness. That is of course if you are used to seeing phantom canines wandering along dark lonely roads in the rural areas of Rhode Island.

Buck Hill Road is off of Route 100. Take Interstate Route 295 to Exit 7, Greenville. Follow Route 44 into Burrillville and then bear right onto Route 100 until you see Buck Hill Road.

# Sherman Plot

The Sherman Cemetery is at a crossroads separated by a large tree. Raised up from the road by a stone wall, the unmarked plot holds the remains of four members of the Sherman family and what looks like the remains of a cellar hole where their cabin once stood.

No records of their deaths are recorded in the historical registers for the state. The cemetery is listed in the state historical records as 001. This means that the Shermans buried their own and kept no record of exact plots. It is known that Clark Sherman is buried there with, some say, his three wives, Ellen, Caroline, and Laura. Others claim it is his one wife, Laura, his daughter, and the daughter's aunt. The state seems to believe the latter. Whatever the case, the spirit of Laura does not remain at rest. If you circle her interment three times during the full moon and call out her name, her spirit will appear. It is said to hover over her grave silently and quiescent before vanishing into the night. Some say it has even spoken faint words of discontent, probably towards the condition of her final resting place. Many of the Burrillville residents say that they have been startled or even frightened by someone they believe is Laura standing at the edge

All that remains of the gravestones at the Sherman lot.

of the plot looking at the road as they have driven by. When they looked back, the ghost was gone.

If you go there do not look for monuments, for all that remains is the base of one gravestone and some indentations in the ground.

The small plot is located at a crossroad with Wakefield Road off Buck Hill Road. Take Route 44 to Route 100, to Buck Hill Road, and Wakefield Road will be on the left.

# The Indian Ghost of
# Hannah Franke

The ghost of a Nipmuc Indian named Hannah Franke endlessly roams the Tarkiln woods in search of her lost love and her prized necklace. She was a nineteen-year-old housekeeper to the Warmsley brothers, who were Nipmuc as well. The Nipmuc Indians and the white settlers lived together in the little hamlet of Tarkiln, which was at the time, called Oak Valley. It was founded around 1700 by John Smith, who later brought his family to this beautiful land. Their first industry was a tar kiln to make pitch and charcoal. The area steadily grew and by 1815 Tarkiln boasted four mills, a tannery, and a gristmill along with 200 settlers in the village. The Nipmucs were not too pleased by this rapid growth. They continued to live in harmony with the white man and his ways despite their feelings. Some even adopted the settler's ways by working in the factories and building houses. Others, although adopting some of the necessities, still despised the way of the white man. It can be told that the Warmsley brothers were among those who held that ideal.

A peddler named John Burke often came down from Vermont to sell his wares in the bustling little mill village. He appeared at the door of the Warmsley home and Hannah Franke answered it. He immediately fell in love with the young Indian girl and a courtship followed.

Each visit, he would bring a token of his affection for her. On one such visit he gave her a beautiful shell necklace in which became her most prized possession. On September 18, 1831, Burke proposed to Hannah and they made preparations to return to Vermont together to marry. This angered the Warmsley brothers, who were opposed to the "mixed" relationship. Hannah gave no attention to their ranting and raving about her going away with Burke to marry and packed her belongings to embark on a new life. This new life was short-lived.

As the couple rode down Log Road, they were accosted at the intersection of Horse Head Trail by the two brothers. Burke tried to avert the brothers so Hannah could flee for safety but was caught and beheaded with an axe. They then caught up to Hannah and killed her with a single shotgun blast. During her struggle, the beloved necklace was ripped from her and lost. The brothers buried the bodies at the crossroad to hide their evil deed but were caught. The younger brother (name unknown) died before justice could prevail after falling from a wagon. Amasa Warmsley was hanged on June 1, 1832, for the murder of John Burke. Hannah was never mentioned.

She has been witnessed ever since the fateful day searching the woods endlessly for her lost love and her necklace and is known to cry for justice in her killing as well. Residents have seen her ghost at various hours of the day and night wandering the edge of the woods near Horse Head Trail and Log Road. One witness, Beth Williams, was terrified at the sighting. She was with her cousin walking the trail when they encountered the specter. It started to run then vanished into thin air near the road. Was her ghost reliving that fateful day?

One day as I stood taking pictures of the area I heard a voice from right behind me. I turned quickly only to catch a glimpse of what people

The intersection of Horse Head Trail and Log Road where Hannah Franke and John Burke were murdered and buried.

call a "shadow person" move out of the corner of my eye. I must admit the voice startled me. It said something like "My justice." Maybe it was Hannah saying, "My necklace." Although the voice was distinct, it happened so fast that I could not catch the exact phrase. In any case, she is now a permanent fixture forever doomed to roam the woods seeking the person and thing that gave her love, happiness, and sadly, a premature departure ... from the world of the living, at least.

Take Interstate Route 295 to Exit 8, North Smithfield. Follow Route 7 about six miles to Tarkiln Road. Take a left onto Tarkiln Road, then a left onto Nichols Road. At the fork, bear right and just before the towers is the Woonsocket Gun Club where the couple was ambushed at the crossroad.

# Zambarano Hospital

Zambarano Hospital is located in the Northwest section of the town. Like all hospitals, it has seen its share of miracles and tragedies. The incidents that surround such institutions make them vulnerable to all kinds of haunting.

This particular hospital hosts an apparition that walks the halls in an old-fashioned style uniform from the nineteenth century. Many frightened patients and staff have witnessed the specter make her nightly rounds. No one knows if she was a dedicated nurse or an ill-fated patient. She appears between the hours of 11:00 PM and 1:00 AM in the south corridor of the hospital. I was once in a band with a person who worked at the hospital. He said many of the staff had seen the ghost and would not venture down that corridor during the witching hours without the presence of another body to keep them company. That was some years ago. Maybe the nurses have gotten used to their extra occupant by now. I kind of doubt it though.

Zambarano Hospital is located on Route 100 in the village of Pascoag. Take Route 44 to Route 100. Go past Buck Hill Road to Wallum Lake. The hospital is on the lake.

# Charlestown

## Great Swamp

Great Swamp is an area where a giant massacre took place on December 19, 1675, between the Narragansett Indians and colonists during the early days of King Philip's War. The Indians were not prepared for the advanced weaponry of the colonists. They were severely overpowered. The brutal battle almost totally annihilated the Narragansett tribe. There is a great burial ground where the Indians were interred and at night you can hear the battle cries, gunshots, and screaming echoing through the hours of darkness as the spirits of those who perished in the struggle relive their last mortal moments.

The area is used for hiking and scouting. In the fall and winter months, hunters grace the woodland looking for game. There is a long catwalk that runs over the swamp where you can almost imagine the treacherous conditions the warriors from both sides had to endure, in many cases, their last mortal moments on earth. There have been many artifacts of the battle unearthed over the centuries such as arrowheads and musket balls. To make things more spine chilling, the ghosts of many of these Indians have also been seen wandering throughout the swamp in full war paint and battle clothing. An obelisk has been set up in the management area commemorating the pivotal struggle of the war. Hunters, hikers, and park service people all swear to the unearthly phenomena lurking among the thickets within these cursed woods. The area is open Monday through Friday, 8:30 to 4:30. Entering the domain after dark is absolutely not recommended.

Take Interstate Route 95 to Route 2 South and follow to Route 138. Take Route 138 to Great Neck Road. Bear left into Great Swamp Management Area.

## Burdick Cemetery

Located at the edge of Burlingame Wildlife Management Area, this historic cemetery boasts disembodied voices, glowing orbs, and even phantom specters that have been witnessed at all hours. Many fishermen and hunters have been spooked by the apparitions and voices within the walls of the cemetery. A customer of my father's tackle shop told me that one morning they were up by the cemetery before dawn camping out on opening day of hunting season. He saw something glowing inside the cemetery and thought it was some vandals or fellow sportsmen. When he approached the graveyard he was immediately frightened at the sight of a glowing transparent shape that resembled a human form standing among the stones. As he told me his story, his eyes widened as if he was reliving that unnerving moment he became a believer in the paranormal. He has not since gone back there, even though the game hunting is to die for.

The cemetery is located on Buckeye Brook Road about 25 yards from the intersection of Shumankanuc Hill Road. Take Interstate Route 95 to Route 1 to King's Factory Road. Stay straight onto Shumankanuc Hill Road then bear left onto Buckeye Brook Road.

Main monument in Burdick cemetery.

Another view of the haunted cemetery.

# Coventry
## Gorton's Funeral Home—
## The Dead Do Not Rest

The "Morgue." It was once Gorton's Funeral Home. It is now home to many restless spirits.

Right down the road from the present Gorton's Funeral Home is a large building on the opposite side of the road. This was the original site of the funeral parlor. I spent several years in this building so I can relate in fine detail all of the strange paranormal experiences that took place there. Here is my story.

This decrepit three-story structure was the first Gorton's Funeral Home until shortly before the middle of the twentieth century, when they moved to the more modern facility up the street from the decaying temporary dwelling of the departed.

Abandoned and dilapidated for almost a half century, this building stood ominously towering over the street. The brick sidewalk was the only boundary between it and the pavement it overshadowed. The "Morgue" as we came to call it, came into our hands when we were searching for a place to rehearse with our band. A group of us were able to rent the cellar for a reasonable fee and began to make it rehearsal ready. The only other occupant became an antique bookstore shortly after we had moved in. Soon, though, the proprietor was off to Florida for better things and we were the sole inhabitants of the whole abode.

The atmosphere of the place was eerie even in the rays of daylight. We would enter through the large doors the deceased were transported through on their way to the embalming table. The place had become unkempt with the passage of time. There was a bathroom with shelves full of embalming fluids and other apothecaries of the last century. The wide stairs allowed for the coffins to be carried by the pallbearers on their way to the spacious viewing rooms of the second and third floors. Just having to climb them gave one a shiver of the brief mortality we suffer and how we would too one day traverse these stairs in a different shroud. The remains of the elevator shaft, crumbled and in dangerous repair sat impetuously at the southern wall. The elevator was added in the 1920s for ease of operation but now posed a threat to anyone who would dare venture within these walls after dark without the aid of a light.

Laced across the massive rooms were a few couches and artifacts of the dead. Clothing trunks and wheelchairs from the nineteenth century lay askew among the rubble and rodents. Canes and other aids of the bygone era sat strewn among the dust that permeated one's lungs when they chose to jar the long resting fine soil.

Any hour was unnerving to walk the looming corridors but mostly at night when the small lamps cast but a faint, uncanny glow upon the massive walls and ceilings where shadows of nightshades could almost be seen dancing in the feeble luminescence of the substandard glow. Some rooms had no electricity at all, making them even more of a mysterious cryptogram to behold after the safety of day had waned away.

One night as I entered the eerie building through the usual double doors, I noticed a strange man coming towards me. He strolled right past me as I stood on the small staircase descending into the cellar and walked right through the old furnace seven feet in front of me!!!

Another incident involved two friends and myself one late night when rehearsal had expired and we were capping up for the night. A figure of a man dressed in baggy clothing, definitely not from this century, appeared in the middle of the room and walked right through the partition we had erected to seal our practice space.

Another night we were constantly being interrupted by crashing and banging coming from a little room just outside of our practice space. Every investigation proved futile, yet the discord continued through the night despite us locking the chamber each time we left it.

One night I left the Morgue from the upper door where a wooden staircase had been erected. As I turned around to secure the door, the figure of a small man wearing glasses and a gloomy gray suit appeared out of the darkness and shoved the door shut from the other side. The specter had a solid stone face with no solace as he gazed at me from the other side of the windowpane for about six seconds before fading into thin air before my eyes. I would later explore the old office only to discover that the face I saw several nights before was the same countenance gracing the antiquated portrait on one of the walls. It was one of the original undertakers of the funeral home.

One of our taping sessions was interrupted by the boom of the double doors leading to our rehearsal space/former embalming room/recording studio. When we replayed the tape to see if the recorder had picked up the possible nuisance, we heard to our astonishment, not only the doors rushing open but the wailing and pleading of a female's voice as well. Yet, as usual, the doors were locked.

Frightful shrieks and unearthly moans would saturate the confines of the sepulture at all hours as if history was replaying the mourning of passed loved ones. One night three of us crept up to the third floor to see who was screaming tumultuously. It was such a clamor that we heard it from the basement. When we reached the large open room, we flicked on the light. The only concrete elements present in the massive expanse to greet us were an old couch, a clothing trunk (filled with clothing of the dead who would have their garments picked out for burial), and a few boards. The screaming stopped the very moment the light illuminated the chamber. There was only one way out and that was the way we came. The elevator shaft was open but yielded a forty foot drop to rocks, rubble, and a piece of the mechanical gear that once helped it to function.

On many occasions we saw the lights turn themselves on and off with no human hand to guide them. At least fifteen people reported ghostly noises or had seen something beyond explanation in the massive morgue. Tape players would shut themselves off as would amplifiers in the middle of songs. Microphones vaulted from their stands as if some veiled energy force was pulling them from the clips and flinging them.

Soon the building was sold and renovations began on the decrepit interior. Even the carriage house behind the building where the horse drawn hearses reposed was made into a woodworking shop for the new owner.

Only the outside remains untouched and as eerie looking as the day I first laid eyes upon it. If you drive by the building, you will have no doubt that you have found the right place.

As for the ghostly encounters, well, they still continue to this day amidst the new walls and ceilings that gave new life to a dying funeral home.

Both buildings are located at 700 Washington Street (Route 117) West off Interstate Route 95 or left at the end of Route 116 South for about one half of a mile.

# Nathanael Greene Homestead

Nathanael Greene was General George Washington's right hand man. He was second-in-command of our armed forces during the Revolutionary War. When the war was over he returned to his hometown of Coventry, Rhode Island, to live out his days. His simple homestead sits along a back street among newer houses. It is now a museum for all to glimpse upon the relics of the past, including some ghosts of the past as well.

Doors like to slam shut within the house and cold spots follow visitors throughout the rooms. People working at the homestead have heard footsteps in the upper floors or adjacent rooms even though there was no one else in the house at the time. It appears that the Greene family still wants their presence known for some reason or another. The curators have yet to see old Nathanael himself. They said they would defiantly ask him why he is still "living" among the living.

The house is at 50 Taft Avenue just over the Coventry/West Warwick line. Take Interstate Route 95 to 117 West. Take a left onto Laurel Avenue to Taft Avenue. For more information, call (401) 821-8630

# George B. Parker Woodland—
# The Trail of Mysterious Cairns

Many former inhabitants of this area left some compelling remnants behind for history and seekers of the paranormal to try and sort out. The land was purchased from the Narragansett Indians in 1642. The Waterman family obtained the land in 1672. The land stayed in the family until Caleb Vaughn obtained the property in 1760. It eventually came into the possession of George Parker through a will. Parker later gave the land to the Audubon Society. After his death in 1946, more property, including the Isaac Bowen house from the early eighteenth century was given to the society for public use.

The Isaac Bowen house is not the only house in the woodland. The remains of another farm sit off of Biscuit Hill Road. The road got its name during the Revolutionary War when a wagon headed for General Rochambeau's camp overturned, spilling biscuits over the hillside.

The foundation of the old farmhouse is claimed haunted by witnesses who have traversed that far into the woods. Claims of voices emanating

One of the many mysterious cairns that lace the George Parker Woodland trail.

out of nowhere within the home's perimeter have spooked more than one hiker. This may seem a bit less thrilling, but the most eerie part of the woodland is at the beginning of the trail.

Mysterious "cairns" lace a section of the Woodland trail. Archeologists have no explanation for the origin of these strategically placed stone mounds. It is reported that strange noises and energy fields emanate from the area. People also get the feeling that they are being watched as they pass through the sparse woods where the many cairns lay. A cairn is a stone mound thought to be a Viking tomb marker. Some think they go as far back as 800 B.C. when the Iberian-Celtic people and the Phoenicians were sailing to present-day America. Whoever built them stayed here for a while because they are scattered throughout New England.

My visit to the site proved to me that what others said held true. Yes there was a feeling of being watched and yes the area of the cairns does emit energy as witnessed from the use of an EMF meter. This is used to measure the amount of electrical energy an object or area has. Whether it is the cairns directly or just the area itself is left up to your judgment. Pay a visit yourself and see if you feel the energy of the dead within the burial mounds.

The preserve is located off Route 102 (Victory Highway) on the Coventry/Foster line. Take Interstate Route 295 to Exit 6, Route 6 West. Follow Route 6 to the intersection of Route 102. Take Route 102 South. Bear onto Maple Valley Road and Parker Woodland is well marked.

# The Floating Coffin

If you happen to be passing through the little hamlet of Hope Village in Coventry, you might cross over the Jackson Bridge spanning the Pawtuxet River. It is at that point you could actually observe a most terrifying spectacle. A black coffin with lit candles on it floating down the river.

One man witnessed the eerie apparition around midnight while crossing the bridge. At first he saw a faint glow coming toward him on the water. As the light drew closer to him, the astonished chap saw that it was a coffin with two candles alit upon it. When he rushed to the nearest home, they all went back to the scene but the apparition was gone. One month later two other people saw the strange coffin bobbing in the flow of the river with candles alit as they too crossed the bridge. They ran to the riverbank and hoisted rocks at the entity. They knocked the candles out but the coffin floated on downstream and out of sight.

It is still seen to the present day, usually around the witching hour of midnight. The origin and destination of the creepy vision remain a complete mystery.

Jackson Bridge is located on Route 115 just off of Route 116 South at the Coventry, Scituate, Cranston, and West Warwick borders. Take Interstate Route 295 to Exit 6,

Route 6 West. Follow to intersection of Route 116. Take a left onto Route 116. Follow to the intersection of Route 115.

# Phenix (Harris) Fire Station

Built in 1887, this edifice also doubled as the village meeting house. Weddings, wakes, and other social gatherings presided within its walls during the early twentieth century. It seems that a few of the revelers from the past centuries have still not left the building.

Visitors and staff alike have felt an uncanny presence in the day room that compels them to make a quick exit from the area. Unrecognizable voices are often heard echoing throughout the building. Many people have seen an apparition pass through the first floor entrance to the stairwell. Personnel of the building frankly swear to all the strange phenomena that have occurred there.

Harris-Phenix is located on the West Warwick/Coventry line on Route 115. Follow the directions above.

# Cranston

## Sprague Mansion

The Sprague manor is arguably one of the most haunted houses in the state of Rhode Island. Many tragedies have unfolded in this eighteenth century homestead. These tragedies have left vexes in the passing of time that now and forever reside in the former estate of the prominent yet tragic family. Here is their story.

William Sprague, who was a very successful entrepreneur, built the manor in 1790. His various mills and bleachery had amassed quite a fortune for his family. William Sprague came to an unfortunate demise when he choked on a fishbone one night during dinner. Doctors tried desperately to remove the bone but he died during the surgery. His son, William, went on to become a United States Senator while his other son, Amasa, tended to the family business. Amasa amassed an even larger fortune from

Sprague Mansion.

Grand ballroom where spirits of the Sprague family have been seen.

the business he inherited. Perhaps he had made a few enemies along the way as well.

On December 31, 1843, Amasa Sprague was found brutally beaten and shot to death near his home. His murder was the result of a long running feud with the Gordon clan, who wanted to put a pub in next to one of the Sprague mills. The Spragues feared it would only create a slack productivity environment within the mill. They were all on the counsel to reject it. John Gordon was hanged for the murder but later Gordon's brother confessed to the crime. This case caused the Rhode Island government to rescind the death penalty.

Amasa was laid out in the living room of the great estate and buried at Swan Point Cemetery, where the massive Sprague memorial now sits. His original stone is on display at the mansion. With the post-Civil War depression, the family fortune dwindled and the mansion was eventually sold. The first ghostly activity seemed to rear its ethereal head around 1925 when an apparition was seen on the staircase. Since that time there have been numerous sightings of the ghost descending the steps of the twenty-eight-room mansion.

In 1966, the Cranston Historical Society obtained the property and restored it as a public building for tours and functions. This has not deterred the many additional ghosts that have been seen in the house since.

Gravestone of Amasa Sprague, now kept at the house. It actually states the fact that he was murdered on the stone.

The mansion now has a number of ghosts roaming its corridors. Along with the wraith on the stairs, witnesses have reported seeing the ghost of Lucy Chase Sprague, who lost a large portion of the family fortune. Other ghosts could be the spirits of William Sprague Sr., who founded the empire and left this world so unexpectedly. Some even claim to see the son of Civil War Governor William Sprague IV, who committed suicide in the house in 1890.

Rhode Island Paranormal Research Group conducted investigations on the property between 2003 and 2004. They claim to have witnessed wraiths reflecting in the glass of a hutch in the ballroom. As they stood in the room, three separate times the image of a man passed by the glass. According to their data collected at the house, the place is extremely active with all kinds of paranormal activity. Hundreds of digital photographs were taken revealing ghosts or paranormal activity in many of the rooms. Pictures of orbs were taken at the scene. Orbs are not a conclusive form of evidence that a place is haunted but the other photos they gathered absolutely confirmed their worst, or maybe in this case, best fears that ghosts roam the mansion at will. One photo even shows the figure of the ghostly woman ascending the famed staircase. Another has images in the ballroom of a lady in what appears to be a long white Victorian dress. Other photos are of misty or wispy white figures, human in form but not recognizable enough to say whose form it might have been. EVP recordings (Electronic Voice Phenomenon) in the house concluded that the living room, ballroom, wine cellar, doll room, and a spare room seem to be active with spirit activity. Even the gift shop was drawn into the spirit's agenda as footsteps were heard there when no one else was around.

Within minutes of entering the house, the EMF meters were going wild. These are used to measure the electrical energy of an area and can tell when paranormal activity is present. These meters coupled with digital thermometers and scanners find cold spots and energy fluxes associated with ghostly encounters.

Ghosts of women, children, and even pets reside within the walls of the estate as witnessed in pictures, videos, and voice recordings taken at the archaic manor. The voice recordings were those of a woman.

Other people through the years have unfortunately, in some cases, met the ghosts of the Sprague mansion. Guests and caretakers alike have stories of covers being pulled off their beds or objects moving without visible hands to guide them. The ghost of a little girl and a dog were seen in one of the bedrooms as well. There is a doll room that is quite unnerving to gaze at. During our visit, although nothing out of the ordinary happened, there was a constant feeling that we were not alone in the house. It was not an unwelcome feeling. After the tour we all mentioned it outside and were quite amazed that we all felt the same way.

Tours are available through the Cranston Historical Society. (401) 944-9226. If you dare…

Sprague Mansion is located on the corners of Dyer Avenue and Cranston Street. Take Interstate Route 95 to Exit 16, Route 10 North. Follow to the Cranston Street exit. Go south on Cranston Street towards Cranston.

# Rhode Island Prison

Guards have seen the apparition of a man jumping off the top of the Maximum Security Building. There are records of suicides within the complex but no one knows for sure who the ghost is. No more information is available, so make what you want of it. The Adult Correctional Institution is located on Pontiac Avenue off of Interstate Route 95.

# The Hanging Tree

There is a dark force associated with this tree, located near the intersection of Fair and Columbia Streets. There is a house next to the tree that is haunted by faces that appear and vanish at random. Cold spots and other paranormal phenomena are associated with the tree, whose limbs hang over the haunted home. The tree was once used as a hanging tree. The people in the neighborhood tend to shun the tree and are afraid to cut it down. It is not really clear if the tree is causing the haunting or the house. No investigations have been made to date of the tree and home. You can visit yourself and draw your own conclusions.

# Cumberland

## The Monastery

Haunts and paranormal activity can reside anywhere there are reason for them, even in places of solace and worship, as you will see as you read on. The present location of the Cumberland Library was once a Monastery. The monks who lived and worked the grounds there have long since moved on. Well, most of them have anyway.

Dom John Murphy purchased 530 acres from the town in 1900 and relocated from Nova Scotia to Cumberland, establishing one of the first Trappist monasteries in the United States. The Monastery of Our Lady of Strict Observance was built between 1902 and 1931. The first building served as a home and place of worship for the entire commune until a church was erected in 1928. The other building was now a guesthouse.

Daily routine was, as one can guess, strictly adhered to. The commune rose early, prayed and meditated, then went to work in the orchards or quarry. Most of the hard work was done by lay brothers who had no wish to become priests. The more pious did God's work. They ate few foods and spoke few words.

In 1950 a fire destroyed the guesthouse and most of the church. The fire started under the stairway of the wooden structure and quickly spread. All of the monks managed to get out safely one way or another. The remains still stand to this day. Although the monks moved to Spencer, Massachusetts, after the fire, some of their brothers have lingered on in the old site.

A monk now haunts the main building, where the library is located. He is said to close or move unattended books. Though no one ever sees the neat servant of good, his knack for tidiness certainly makes itself known. There have been sightings of phantom monks roaming the yards around the buildings as well. Paranormal groups in the area are very interested in this place. The haunting continues to entice those wanting a formal investigation. I'm in. How about you?

The Cumberland Public Library where the ghost of a monk closes books.

The Monastery is located on Route 114 (Diamond Hill Road). Take Interstate Route 295 to Exit 11 towards Central Falls and the site is about 2.5 miles on the right.

# Nine Men's Misery

One of early Cumberland's darkest hours came on the day of March 26, 1676, during the height of King Philip's War. The horrible events that took place are still alive in the memory of all who read about it. The woods are also still alive with the same memory.

Stone tomb of the nine men killed in battle on March 26, 1676.

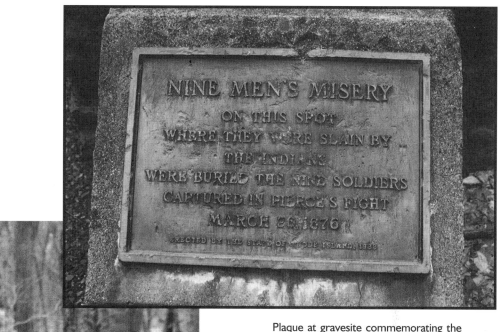

NINE MEN'S MISERY
ON THIS SPOT
WHERE THEY WERE SLAIN BY
THE INDIANS
WERE BURIED THE NINE SOLDIERS
CAPTURED IN PIERCE'S FIGHT
MARCH 28, 1676
ERECTED BY THE STATE OF RHODE ISLAND, 1928

Plaque at gravesite commemorating the tragic incident. Plaque was erected in 1929.

On that fateful Sunday morning Captain Michael Pierce headed a small group of militia in looking for a small raiding party of Indians who had attacked Warwick and Providence. They were supposedly on their way to Attleboro when they met up with Cononchet and his marauders. They were ambushed but held their ground until all hope was lost. At that point they broke ranks and fled for safety. All but nine escaped in the retreat. These captives were taken to a spot in the woods of present day Cumberland and tortured.

According to Native Indian tradition, they were seated on a rock where a fire was lit and a war dance was performed. What exactly happened is not known. Some say they were skinned alive, then hung to die. Afterward they were beheaded and their heads were placed on poles. Other reliable chronicles state that the Indians could not decide on the mode of torture, so they "dispatched their prisoners with a tomahawk."

The latter seems to hold more validity as of an article in the *Providence Journal* dating back to 1886, where a Dr. Bowen and a few men dug up the graves and were pulling the skeletons out when the townspeople stopped them. They were ordered to return the graves to their previous state. Before this, the exact identity of the men buried there was lost to antiquity. Now they knew where the men had hailed from. One skeleton, extraordinary in size and having a double set of teeth, was identified as Benjamin Bucklin who was known to have come from the Rehoboth Militia.

Whichever is the case, help arrived too late to save the men who were found brutally murdered by their captors. They were buried in the spot now called "Nine Men's Misery" and a monument was put up in their honor in 1928, but they do not remain at rest. Visitors to the site have often heard the cries and moans of the men reliving their last agonizing moments. Witnesses have put their ears up to the rocks and have heard the sounds of the men within the tomb. Investigators have brought equipment to the site to measure the EMF levels and were astonished at how high the readings were near the grave. Paranormal seekers have taken some bloodcurdling EVP recordings at the site.

Nine Men's Misery is not the only chilling entity in these woods. There is also the ghost of a little child seen running along the swamp near the monument. A phantom rider appears out of nowhere on the trail and dissolves into thin air just as quickly. Perhaps they were also victims of Indian attacks in revenge for the Great Swamp Massacre a year before. If you are nervous of what might lurk behind the trees, I suggest you visit this particular place in the safety of daylight with a few other friends.

Nine Men's Misery can be found in the woods behind the Cumberland Monastery. See above for directions.

# West Wrentham House

An old man haunts this historical house. He is a very active ghost. He materializes in front of people, bangs on walls, makes strange noises, and even appears in dreams. The present owners think he is a previous owner but they do not know which one. Little else is known, as the historical information is sketchy.

Take Exit 10, Route 122 (Mendon Road) off of Interstate Route 295 to West Wrentham Road. The house should be marked.

# Elder Ballou Meetinghouse Road
## — The Cemetery Man in Grey

Hill where ghost in grey was seen.

Some old cemeteries can make the hair on the back of your neck stand up. This particular cemetery will make every hair on your whole head stand tall. That is, if you are brave enough to enter its gates. This is by far the creepiest cemetery in the whole state.

As expected, it is haunted. A man in a gray uniform walks among the stones only to disappear when confronted or called to. Whether he was a caretaker or a permanent resident of the graveyard is unknown. I personally witnessed this apparition one night. That was what prompted me to go back and take pictures of the cemetery for this book. We were out legend tripping around Halloween. Legend tripping is when you hear about a place and you informally visit it to check things out.

As I stood at the bottom of the little hill with a friend and my wife, my eyes were quickly drawn to movement just ahead of us. There moving slowly among the stones was a figure of a man in a gray suit. You could

More stones along hillside of eerie graveyard.

almost see through him and he had a low ethereal glow about him. We knew he was not of this world. He vanished as soon as he reached the top of the hill. My wife would not go further, so we made a hasty investigation and left the area.

A more formal investigation during daylight hours turned up nothing unusual. But I interviewed a few locals and they filled in the blanks on the other information I now give to you.

Voices whispering out of nowhere are also common in this cemetery. The historical cemetery is where the Ballou family is buried. There are several "keeps" or holding crypts as we know them where the dead were kept until the spring thaw enabled the family to dig up the ground for proper burial.

Cries and moans of sorrow are heard emanating from these keeps. Motorists passing the burial ground can sometimes hear the wailing of the past mourners when their windows are open. Some have stopped to check out the source. Most don't.

Take Route 122 (Mendon Road) to Elder Ballou Meetinghouse Road. The cemetery is about a quarter of a mile in on the left.

# Tower Hill Road

This winding country road is host to numerous ghosts. The ghost of a little girl is most frequently spied sitting in the front yard of an old farmhouse. On the sharpest curve of the road is the spirit of a little boy running with his dog. He was hit and killed there many years ago. Accidents of that nature are common on this dangerous track. A phantom toddler on a tricycle has also been spotted in the woods surrounding the snaking lane. Many people have reported feeling a presence with them while traveling down this road. Some say that a man took a little boy up into the woods with his dog and they never were seen again. That could be the product of urban legend. The other accounts of this paranormal place are defiantly defended by those who have traveled the road on a dark night or even a scenic sunny day.

Tower Hill Road connects Mendon Road with Diamond Hill Road.

# Reservoir Road

The specter of a faceless man has been seen here.

Motorists driving by a desolate spot in the road have been shaken by the frightening spectacle. When they look in their rear view mirror or quickly pull over, they find the apparition has suddenly vanished.

Reservoir Road is off of Diamond Hill Road, Route 114.

# East Providence

## The Haunted Carousel at Crescent Park

Haunted Carousel at former Crescent Park.

The music of an old fashioned carousel conjures up visions of laughing children, the smell of cotton candy, and all the other revelry that gives amusement parks that certain timeless wonder. In the case of the Looff Carousel on the old Crescent Park fairgrounds, when the carousel stops the phantom laughter and music of yesteryear continue to fill the air.

I remember riding the great wooden horses as a child. As I look back now to those moments, I can remember the eerie aura the carousel presented to me. I was strangely drawn to it yet fearfully repelled by the horse's faces that looked so alive and menacing in their demeanor. The wooden steeds had eyes that would follow you, watching to see which one you would pick. Then the music would start and the horses would come to life. You could almost see the snarled grins on their faces as if they were waiting for a child to be thrown from the majestic ride. Perhaps it was just the immense size of the structure in contrast to my smaller frame that was so intimidating. Perhaps it was much more.

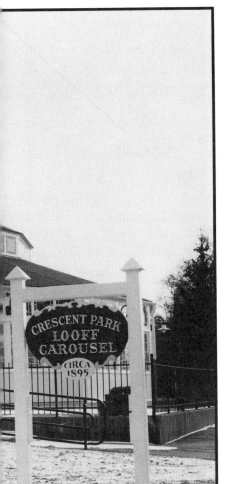

Crescent Park was built in 1886 along the shores of the bay in Riverside (then known as Wannamoisett), Rhode Island. It became known as the "Coney Island of New England" and people flocked from all over the territory to take in the fun and merriment of this lavish amusement park. One of the most beautiful attractions in the park was the great carousel built by Charles I.D. Looff in 1895. The carousel had sixty-two hand carved figures and four chariots surrounding an equally elaborate band organ by A. Ruth and Sohn, also with moving figures.

The park changed hands several times until 1920 when Mr. Looff himself took ownership and expanded the rides and games. He added a ballroom and roller rink. The park saw hard times during World War II and was purchased by the Crescent Park Realty Company. Arthur Simmons and Fred McCusker became the new managers and renovated the antiquated park. The new park prospered once more during the 1950s and 1960s until the park was sold one more time to one Melvin T. Berry.

On September 2, 1969, the ballroom burned to the ground. The park began faltering once more until it was auctioned off in 1979. The carousel was doomed to be dismantled when some residents bought it and refurbished it. The ornate carousel now sits ominously as a National Historic

Horses sit ominously waiting for someone to bring them to life.

Landmark in the same place to this day and is open from Easter to Columbus Day, where seventy-five cents will buy you a ride on the haunted horses. Often, however, the carousel starts up by itself and the lights flicker on and off or the music will start playing when there is no visible hand to turn it on. Many people have also heard the voices of long past patrons permeating the ocean breeze as laughter and merriment once more fill the abandoned amusement park.

There is even the ghost of a woman in a nineteenth century skirt seen looking quietly out over the water as if she is waiting for someone or in deep contemplation of an event that may have changed her life. Such an event may be why she is bound to roam the earth still, forever looking into the great wide ocean. No one knows who she was but my neighbor attests to the strange history and haunts of the park as her grandparents, Albert and Elizabeth Lavoie, worked some of the rides during the 1950s and 1960s. They had many strange accounts to tell her as a youth who also frequented the establishment during the hot Rhode Island summers.

Now the carousel sits along the side of Bullocks Point Avenue. Its towering point can be seen from a good distance away. It is quite a breathtaking sight but even creepier when the lights go on and the music starts within the sealed doors of the building. The horses grin in the most devilish of manners as the ghost children scream and laugh on their eternal ride, trying to grab the brass ring.

I urge you to try a ride on the mysterious carousel. You never know who might pop up beside you.

The carousel is located on Bullocks Point Avenue. Take Interstate 195 to Route 114 South. Follow until it becomes Bullocks Point Avenue. Carousel is on your left.

## Wannamoisett Country Club

Spectral Indian riders haunt the eighteenth fairway of this golf course. When seen, they race towards their victims, only to vanish before any physical contact is made. I could not find any other information on this particular haunt. It could just be a case of urban legend. I will let you be the judge.

The golf course is located on Route 114 in Rumford, East Providence. Follow directions above to Route 114 but go north on Route 114 then take left onto Bent Road at corner of golf course to where the 18th Hole is.

# Exeter

## Chestnut Hill Baptist Church

This cemetery is not only haunted by a few ghosts but also contains the remains of Rhode Island's last vampire. It is said she is one of the phantoms that roam the stones in the misty moonlit nights as well.

Rhode Island was once known as the vampire capital of America. The smallest state in the Union hosted the largest number of reports and accounts of vampirism. It was said that the "undead" would leave their tombs in the dark bowers of the night within the fields and forests of rural Rhode Island to feed upon the blood of the living. Such creatures of the shadows fed solely upon family members during their unearthly visits for fear of being found out. They would then suck the very juice of life out of the ones they held dear in life.

Scores of hysterical families dug up loved ones in the eighteenth and nineteenth centuries looking for the devil's concubine among them. The deceased were disinterred and the ones suspected of vampirism had their hearts cut out and burned. The ashes would then be mixed with medicine and the affected family members would drink the potion to cure them of the vampire's contamination. The body was later laid back in the grave to rest in eternal peace. This was typical New England custom for exorcising a vampire.

There are at least fifteen documented cases throughout our history and probably hundreds more that went unaccounted for.

The last known case of vampirism took place in Exeter in March of 1892 at the place now known as Historical Cemetery #22 behind the Chestnut Hill Baptist Church.

Mercy Brown died on January 17, 1892, of consumption. Her mother and sister, Mary Eliza and Mary Olive, passed away years before from the dreaded disease. Mary Eliza died on December 8, 1883, followed by her daughter, Mary Olive, on June 6, 1884, at age twenty. Mercy fell ill and passed on as well. The ground was too hard from the frost to dig a grave so Mercy was laid in the "Keep" until spring could find a more favorable

The "Keep" where Mercy Brown was kept prior to her being exorcised for vampirism.

burial. A Keep is the name given to those crypts one might see in the old cemeteries of New England. When the ground was frozen it was common for the town to lay the bodies in these crypts for safe keeping until the spring thaw. They also served as storage during the summer months just in case the declaration of their death was premature. Some were equipped with a bell in case the person actually woke up. They could sound the bell to let the townspeople know it was not yet their time.

Her brother, Edwin, then contracted the horrible disease and was wasting away. He went to the famous Colorado Springs to help cure his plight but returned after eighteen months and became more ill than before. The local folk feared vampirism was to blame and in March of 1892, sought permission to dig up the corpses of Mary Olive and Mary Eliza Brown. Mercy, who had not yet been buried, would be the last family member they would check. With the scornful assertion that vampires did not exist, George T. Brown, father of Mercy and the family's patriarch, finally gave in to the pleadings of his neighbors. He would not accompany them to the graveyard when they performed their deed.

With the help of Dr. Metcalf from Wickford presiding, a group of locals dug the bodies up. Both were well on their way to decomposition in the grave yet Mercy, who was being held in the Keep until spring, had not only stayed untainted by death but had also grown hair and nails. This was enough evidence of vampirism for the townsfolk. They cut out her heart and lungs. They then burned them on a rock in the cemetery and fed the ashes to Edwin with medicine. The cure failed and he passed away on May 2, 1892. Accounts of the incident were recorded in the *Providence Journal* and the *Pawtuxet Valley Gleaner* on March 25, 1892. Shortly after this event the rural farmers were enlightened on the dreaded disease tuberculosis, or consumption as they called it and how to better treat it.

The spirit of Mercy is among several ghosts that now haunt the graveyard. The Keep seems to be the center of activity. Tri-State Paranormal Group has stated that a few of the ghosts are those of people who woke up in the Keep but could not sound the alarm for some reason. Therefore they either froze to death or starved. The restless spirits now roam the grounds around the Keep endlessly looking for answers. There are many accounts from newspapers to family who have witnessed eerie phenomena within the burial ground.

Eyewitnesses have not only seen the wraiths but have also heard a woman's cries from among the gravestones. Louis Everett Peck, an descendant of the Brown family, once told the *Providence Journal* of a time when he witnessed a strange light over Mercy's grave in the 1960s. He was eighteen years old at the time and went to visit the grave with his brother David. The great ball of blue light hovering over the Brown plot scared Louis and his brother so much they ran away from the cemetery and never looked back. To this day many people report seeing the blue light over Mercy's grave.

Take Interstate Route 95 to Exit 5, Route 102. Follow Route 102 into Exeter and Chestnut Hill Baptist Church will be on a rise. Pull in the parking lot and the cemetery is right in front of you.

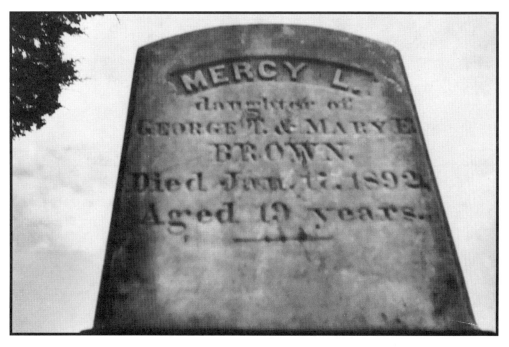

Mercy Brown's final resting place. She was the last of the Rhode Island "vampires."

One of the abandoned buildings at the former Ladd complex.

# Joseph P. Ladd School

Some places are frightful no matter what the hour of the day. In the case of the old abandoned Ladd School, this seems to hold truer than most places I have ever visited. Not only is it extremely haunted, the buildings and trees are twisted and gnarly beyond description. The reason for it being haunting is equally horrible as well.

The Joseph P. Ladd School was founded in 1907 to assist the mentally handicapped. The original name of the facility was the Rhode Island School for the Feeble Minded. It was said that the need for such an institution arose from comments of one Dr. Walter Fernald who in 1893 suggested that these feeble minded people would grow up to become dregs of society.

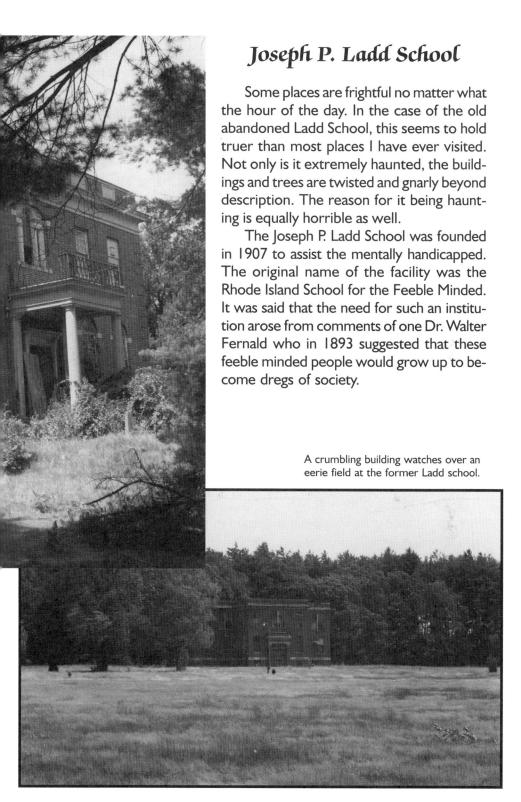

A crumbling building watches over an eerie field at the former Ladd school.

The school actually started out as a farm colony where the people worked in the fields, prepared food, and mended clothing. They lived in little cottages for a while until the girl's dormitory was erected in 1909. In 1917 the name of the school was changed to the Exeter School and the feeble minded was considerately dropped.

By 1928 it had become a haven for all of society's refuse. Poor funding and overcrowding began to take its toll on the quality of life within the complex. Abuse of the patients became a normal routine. On June 1, 1956, Joseph Ladd finally retired as director of the facility.

The stories of abuse seem impossible to fathom. Accounts of patients having teeth pulled without any local anesthetics to save money and other such physical tortures within the infirmary, which featured a padded cell, began to leak out to the patients' families. These discoveries were followed by multitudes of wrongful abuse and death lawsuits. By the 1970s there were many private assistance homes as alternatives to the institution. They also brought human rights suits against the horrible treatment of the helpless patients. In 1986, the state sought to close the facility and by 1993 the doors were sealed for the last time. This did not end the saga of the school, as both spirits of some of the patients revisit and visions of terrible events replay over and over throughout the buildings on the cursed grounds.

There are ten buildings strewn across open fields of overgrown grass. The sight is creepy even in daylight. Gnarled trees surround the whole compound, which is comprised of a recreation building, dormitories, classroom buildings, administration, and community buildings, a chapel, a crematorium, and a six story cylindrical-shaped infirmary containing a padded cell, operating rooms, dental clinic, morgue, and x-ray room. There are incident reports of patients scattered about dating up to 1987, even though the hospital was ordered closed in 1982.

The phenomena include orbs and streaks of light. Hazy figures among the buildings and near the playground have been seen on many occasions. There are photos of orbs and streaks of light in the infirmary. EVP recordings have revealed whispers, cries, and other voices among the buildings. Beds and other items have been moved around where no one could have put them. Eerie noises in the hallways like the sound of someone dragging something have also been heard. A camera was knocked out of a woman's hands by an unseen force when she went to take a photo of one of the buildings. As she went to pick it up, it was smacked from her hands again. The shadows roaming the area have been known to actually confront those who are brave enough to enter the compound. It is reported that icy cold wind blows across the meadows between the buildings even on the calmest of days.

Our investigation of the school was somewhat uneventful. We were able to capture some good pictures but no ghostly activity was going on at that time. The only thing we encountered was the feeling of being watched from a few of the buildings as we moved about the complex.

The area is off limits to the public at present due to construction, so heed the warnings and get permission to enter the facility. It is right next to the Veterans Memorial Cemetery on Allentown Road off of Route 4. Follow directions above to get to Route 4.

# Historical Cemetery #14

Historical Cemetery #22 hosts the last of the Rhode Island vampires. But, it is Historical Cemetery #14, just a few miles away that contains the remains of the Tillinghast family. Their story is the first written accounts of vampirism in the state.

Stutley Tillinghast, an apple farmer by trade, was said to have had a dreadful dream in which he lost half of his orchard. Even though the dream disturbed him dearly, he plodded on with his daily routine. It was not very long after the dream that his daughter, Sarah, the oldest girl of his fourteen children, became ill with consumption. Consumption is what the rural folk once called tuberculosis. She died in 1790 at the age of fourteen. Soon after her burial, his other children began to show signs of the terrible disease.

One by one they wasted away while he and his wife helplessly watched. Each child deliriously uttered in frightful recollection how Sarah was visiting them at night, taking away the very life they clung to so desperately. The children died one after another at such a pace that poor Stutley did not have the time or provisions to acquire proper headstones. They were buried side by side with fieldstone markers until a time when appropriate monuments could be made for his beloved children. When the sixth child fell ill and complained of Sarah coming back from the grave at night to visit her, the townsfolk had no doubt the deaths were the work of a vampire.

A group of neighbors along with the Tillinghasts went to the family plot where they unearthed the bodies of the children. Even though a relatively short time had passed since their deaths, they were all well on their way back to the earth. All but Sarah, who was the first to be buried. Not only was she in good condition, when they cut her open they found fresh blood in her heart. The townspeople had found their vampire.

They cut her heart out and burned it, then fed the ashes to the youngest child with medicine. The sixth child died despite of the concoction that was meant to cure her. It was concluded she was too ill to save. Stutley's dream of losing half his orchard was fulfilled as the unfortunate farmer lost half of his children.

To this day there are six unmarked fieldstone gravesites side by side that are most likely those of the children who died so hastily in a row. There is also a large stone with the initials "ST" carved in it next to the stone of his wife, Honor Tillinghast. This is most likely the stone of Stutley himself, suggesting they never got to have a proper stone made for him either. Stonecutters were far and few between and it was a time consuming task, especially during the time when consumption took so many people in New England so prematurely to their graves. There is another headstone with the name Stutley Tillinghast engraved on it, but the birth date is c.1775 and the date of death is March 13, 1848. This would suggest he was the son of the man whose dream was a foretelling of great tragedy and loss.

More accounts of vampires would soon create a wave of panic for the next century to come before the scare subsided. Or has it …

The cemetery sits on Forest Hills Drive, which is across from Tripp's Corner Road on Route 102, just about a mile from Chestnut Hill Baptist Church.

The Tillinghast children died so fast there was no time or money for proper burial markers. They were buried in succession and dug up the same way. No one knows what child rests under what grave marker, as they never got a chance to purchase proper stones.

# Foster

## Ramtail Factory— Rhode Island's Officially Haunted Landmark

Deep in the woods of Foster, Rhode Island, along an old road lies the remains of the Ramtail Factory. This once thriving woolen factory was Foster's largest attempt at a waterwheel driven mill of the type so prominent in its day. Now just stone foundations, the area still marks its place in time as Rhode Island's only officially haunted site as recognized in the 1885 State Census (page 36).

If one is traveling down Route 6 West from Providence, you will soon come to the Historical Hopkin's Mill District. Ramtail Road cuts across the thoroughfare and just before the bridge, on your left, you will see a field where the old road picks up to this most haunted locality. But! Dare not venture in alone or after the sun's rays have fallen beyond where earth meets the sky ... for darkness cloaks the area with a sinister, uncanny pith. It is there, in the eerie darkness, where the sounds of footsteps and the swinging of an old lantern can be heard as the ghost of Peleg Walker makes his eternal rounds, watching over the now decrepit ruins of the factory he had guarded in life.

The factory was originally founded by William Potter as a fulling mill in 1799. Local farmers took their wool to be cleaned and prepared for cloth. It wasn't until 1813, when Potter bought more land to the south of the mill, that he took on a partner and expanded the operation. That partner was his son-in-law, Peleg Walker. Together they established the Foster Woolen Factory, more appropriately known as the Ramtail Factory, along the banks of the Ponagansett River.

It was now dedicated to weaving and spinning cloth. Every day wagons rolled over the little bridge that traversed the river laden with deliveries to and from the bustling complex. William Potter ran the business by day and Peleg was given the task of night watchman. As soon as the twilight hours reached the land, there was Peleg Walker, lantern in hand, sauntering from building to building keeping the night's concerns in harmony. When the sun began to rise, he would then finish his shift by ringing the large bell of the factory that beckoned the workers into their morning toils. It was a good partnership ... until one day ...

Potter and Walker had a dispute. There is no written record of what the argument was about, although it was said to be over money. Whatever happened, it was also known that the disagreement had enough impact on Peleg that he was quoted as saying that they would some day soon have to take the keys to the mill from a dead man's pocket.

His promise was fulfilled when, on the morning of May 19, 1822, the echo of the work bell failed to permeate the air. The curious workers, along with Mr. Potter, arrived at the mill only to find it locked up. They broke into the main building where a grisly spectacle awaited them. There, hanging from the bell rope, was Peleg Walker. In the pocket of the thirty-five-year-old Walker were the keys to the factory.

He was given a Christian burial in the family plot overlooking what is now Hopkin's Mill Pond. Everything could continue as before, or so they thought.

A few nights later, the bell began tolling at the stroke of midnight. The awakened little hamlet apprehensively approached the mill. When they entered the building, the strange tolling ceased. After a search turned up nobody else in the structure, it was once again secured for the night.

The pealing of the bell filled the air again the next night at the witching hour and, as before, with no evidence of foul play. The Potters, now in dismay, removed the rope but this did not stop Peleg from his nightly concert. The phantom ringing invaded the dead of night once again and the Potters were forced to remove the bell once and for all.

One night, however, the villagers were awoken by a frightful disquiet. It was the mill running full tilt. The frightened inhabitants ogled in disbelief as the factory ran by its own volition. Every wheel, spindle, and loom was turning at full tilt. Even the giant water wheel used to run the mill was turning *opposite the flow of the stream!!!* When the same incident took place a few nights later, the workers began to leave the cursed grounds for fear of their lives.

The ghost of Peleg Walker was soon to be seen by a few men walking by the factory one night. They witnessed the glowing nightshade walking about the mill buildings with a lantern in its hand. The men knew by its distinctive features that it was the spirit of Peleg Walker.

By now the struggling business was too far in debt to continue. No one would work in a haunted factory where the specter had hung himself. By 1850, the Ramtail Factory was no longer open. The factory's demise is credited to the haunting of Peleg Walker in the *Foster Historical Records* book in the Rhode Island Historical Library. The whole mill complex was

A section of wall at the Ramtail Factory.

Another section of the factory where the wagons were kept as evidenced by remnants of springs, hitches, and wheels found in the area of the photo.

57

burned to its foundations in the 1880s by an immense blaze. It is these very foundations that still sit portentously in the thicket of Foster even as you read this narrative.

My investigations with the ghostly site began on a fall day in 1993 when a friend and I visited the site via the old road that still runs a passage through the forest. After crossing over the remnants of the old bridge, (now a flooded out beaver dam) we came upon the ruins. Laid out precariously were several foundations and some small rusty artifacts. One foundation was very large in area. This was the main building. We now knew what to expect on our late night return.

It wasn't until several vigils that we witnessed a most hair raising spectacle. My friend John and I stood on the old road overlooking the main foundation when it happened! About forty-five minutes had passed when we witnessed a glowing oblong ball of light emerge from behind the trees and hover in the air within the foundation. It stirred about within the foundation for about forty seconds, then continued on its way back into the trees. Later I would realize that the specter of light was hovering at the height of what was once the first floor of the factory.

Another nightly visit turned a few skeptics into trembling believers. As we stood in the eerie blanket of darkness, there slowly came near the sound of a lantern swinging to and fro. Now it was right beside us. It passed by us and began returning towards us again yet there was no visible form to be seen carrying the phantom torch as the creaking filled our ears, causing the very hair on our necks and arms to stand tall. Another night at the coveted sight would give me the same show as before. Peleg was still making his rounds in the old factory just as he did in life. All were truly convinced that the Ramtail Factory is genuinely haunted.

Other eyewitness accounts include Mark Dirrigl who visited the woods in 2001 after reading an article I had written on the ghost. He arrived just as the sun was waning and meandered through the ruins taking recordings and photos. When darkness had taken its toll on the land, he set up his camera and waited for Mr. Walker to show. He would not be disappointed. As he sat there in the woods, he suddenly heard the creaking of a lantern swinging to and fro. He could almost feel the presence move past him even though there was no visible entity. He wrote about his experience in the October 2001 issue of *FATE* magazine. He would later have his pictures developed and discover the image of a white oblong streak of light in one of the frames.

Glenn Hopkins, a lifelong resident of Foster, who maintains that along the old road he has not only seen the lantern glow but has also heard the bell peal at the hour of midnight. As he stated to me, "Twice I have heard the bell ring, once when I was twelve and another time when I was nineteen. It sounded eerie and mournful." Old timers say it would ring quite often, especially during a full moon. His grandmother told many a tale of the ghost of Peleg Walker, who walked the old carriage lane, then called Rounds Hill Road with his spectral light in hand.

We all think that Peleg still makes his eternal rounds of the place he so loved in life. On his stone the inscription reads, "Life how short. Eternity how long." Has he been fated to follow those very words forever by

The weather beaten grave of Peleg Walker in the Potter family plot.

haunting the site where he took his life? If so, then Ramtail Factory will always be guarded by its watcher and, even if you don't see him, one visit and you will be easily convinced that the factory is indeed still alive and full of spirit.

To get to the remains of the mill, take Interstate Route 295 to Exit 6, Route 6 West. Follow Route 6 into Foster and turn left onto Ramtail Road, where the cemetery is on your left. Just before the little bridge on the left is a field that runs along the brook. Follow the brook and you will pick up the old road that will lead you to the river where the beaver dam was. Go over the river and the remains of the factory are one hundred yards or so on both sides of the road.

# Dolly Cole Brook

When I was a child, my father and I always went fishing in the Foster area. One of his favorite places was Dolly Cole Brook. I cannot tell you how many times I tried my luck in the stream in hopes of catching the elusive trout that roamed the waters but I can tell you of one time that would later become etched into my memory even to this day.

I was about eleven years old when we were at the brook fishing in the late afternoon. My father wandered downstream a short way and I stayed near a small pool. Suddenly there was a reflection in the water and standing across the pool from me was the figure of a young woman. She appeared out of nowhere. I never even heard her feet crunching in the leaves as she approached. I turned my head to see if my father was nearby and when I turned back in her direction, she was gone. I always thought this was an odd occurrence but never really put much else into it until one day three years later.

As I read the Halloween issue of the local newspaper, I noticed a story on Dolly Cole who was found murdered near the very brook that now bears her name. This is when it all came together in my head. Had I seen a real ghost a few years ago? I was kind of excited over the fact and soon would learn the tale of this haunted area.

Dorothy Ellen Cole, aged twenty-seven at the time of her death, was found in the woods of Foster in 1893. There exists only a small clipping of the incident followed by an obituary. Any other records of the case were lost in a great fire that consumed the hall of records in the 1930s.

Although the records are long gone, her ghost still shows up in the wooded area where she was found quite frequently. Tucker Hollow Road is a dirt lane that traverses the peculiar section of woods. Along the road there is a stream and a small glade where Dolly Cole's body was discovered. It is in this area where the spirit of

Dolly Cole Bridge, where her ghost is sometimes seen by the flowing waters of the brook that also bears her name.

Dolly Cole roams the woods near a swamp and the bridge that is named in memory of her.

Scores of hikers, hunters, and fishermen all claim to have witnessed the young ghost. She is described as a young brunette with long flowing hair in nineteenth century farm clothing. She will suddenly appear in the woods near them looking very much alive until she vanishes in the wink of an eye.

Maybe she is endlessly looking to identify the person who is responsible for her untimely demise. The Swamp where she is frequently seen is now the property of the Cranston Fish and Game Association. Permission to go into that area would be deemed necessary as there might be hunters lurking about. The bridge, however, is accessible to all and is another hot spot for sightings.

Take Route 6 to Hopkins Mill District into the historic area marked by signs. Tucker Hollow Road off Route 6 in the Hopkins Mill District. The Bridge is on Route 6 at the bottom of Dolly Cole Hill.

# The Ghost Lot of
# Tucker Hollow Road

The spirit of Aunt Lonnie Davis (or Lannie) is reported to still roam the field where her house once stood. Lonnie Davis was a reclusive old woman who shunned her neighbors. This led to the local denizens to fear her as a witch. She was certainly a spectacle to behold. The old woman would take her wheelbarrow to the town store, fill it up with provisions, and then walk it up and down the tiring hills of Danielson Pike to her home on Tucker Hollow Road. Not even the most polite of gentry was ever given opportunity to lend a hand to the old spinster. This really caused the townsfolk to steer clear of her.

Before she died, Aunt Lonnie swore to them that she would never rest so long as even two boards remained nailed together on her house. She never wanted her home to go to any of the people who referred to her as a minion of the devil.

Time passed and so did she but she did not go away. Whenever someone entered the property, noises would emanate from the empty structure. Whispers of warning would sound in their ears as well as a cold breath blowing down their neck.

The neighbors soon realized she was not leaving until her wish was fulfilled. They dismantled the house board by board as she requested. Not a single slat remained fastened to another. Some claim her spirit still remains where the old house was, eternally watching over her property that was never rebuilt upon.

Take Route 6 to Tucker Hollow Road. The field is just down the road in a clearing behind a few trees. The locals have dubbed it the "Ghost Lot."

## Jencks Road—Another Vampire

Along the Connecticut border, sitting unassuming behind newer houses, is the remains of another incident in the vampire plague that once afflicted Rhode Island.

Captain Levi Young and Annie Perkins Young settled in Foster and started a family. The first to be born was Nancy. They then had several other children. When Nancy grew suddenly ill, they thought she had contacted a cold. As the symptoms grew worse, they knew she had consumption and there was nothing they could do to save her. Nancy died on April 26, 1827, at only nineteen years of age. She was buried in the family plot on the farm.

When a second daughter, Almira, became ill, Captain Young began to fear the worst. Soon more of his children came down with the illness and complained of strange delusions. After countless doctors failed to cure the disease that was slowly taking the Young family to their graves, he had only one answer left. He, along with friends and neighbors, determined that Nancy was a vampire feeding on the lifeblood of the family. They exhumed her body in the summer of 1827 and burned it while the family stood around inhaling the smoke as a remedy for the dreaded sickness afflicting them. This was to no avail as several more children including Almira succumbed to the horrible disease.

The Young cemetery is located off Jencks Hill Road. Take Route 6 to Cucumber Hill Road at the Connecticut border. Take a left and then right on Plain Woods Road. Take a left onto Jencks Hill Road from there. The cemetery is in the woods and difficult to spot.

# Moosup Valley Bridge
## and Cemetery

The specter of a man carrying a broken shovel is seen walking along the road near the bridge and cemetery. He has also been spotted standing in front of the Grange Hall just down the street from the bridge. There is no information on who the spectral worker might be. It is accepted belief that he was once a gravedigger for the cemetery he is seen near and still holds his position, even though he is now in the spirit world.

Moosup Valley is in western Foster near the Connecticut border. Take Interstate Route 295 to Exit 6, Route 6, Hartford. Follow to Connecticut border. Take a left onto Cucumber Hill Road just before the border. Follow Cucumber Hill Road to Moosup Center. Bear left onto Moosup Hill Road. The bridge and cemetery are straight ahead.

# Glocester
## Stagecoach Tavern—
## Fine Food and Spirits of All Kinds

Chepachet Village is alive with history: From the shooting of Betty, America's second pachyderm on the Chepachet Bridge to the oldest continually running store in all of the USA. It also has some of the finest antiques for sale in the whole country and was the scene of the Dorr Rebellion, where the right to form independent political parties in this country was born.

This little hamlet sits along Route 44 in the northern part of Rhode Island. Its quaint antique shops and historical buildings have brought many tourists and shoppers far back in time. It has also managed to bring the people from far back in time to our era.

The Stagecoach Tavern in Glocester, Rhode Island

The building that hosts the most ghosts in the area is the Stagecoach Tavern. The tavern was built in the eighteenth century as a stage stop for the weary travelers of the Providence-Hartford stage run. The people would dine and lodge there while fresh horses were exchanged for the next leg of the route. The atmosphere and cuisine to this day are still second to none.

In 1842 it was the scene of the Dorr Rebellion. Thomas Dorr of the newly formed People's Party was elected governor but Samuel King refused to step down. A struggle ensued and King's troops marched down Route 44 towards the awaiting Dorr army on Acote's Hill just down the road from the tavern. Dorr saw he was vastly outnumbered and dispersed his troops. He fled to nearby Connecticut.

King's troops lodged the summer at the tavern, nearly bankrupting the owner, Jedediah Sprague, who was never compensated by the state for their gluttonous pleasures. The only casualty of the rebellion was when someone fired shots through the keyhole of the front door, hitting Horace Bordeen in the thigh. As time graced this building, so did the ghosts that began to make their mark in the walls of the ancient inn.

Among the many spirits of the tavern is the ghost of a woman who appears in the corner booth of the dining room. She is seen in nineteenth century dress and appears at random.

Eva-Marie Belheumer, a long time employee of the restaurant, has seen many other things. On one occasion she walked into the kitchen past a figure standing near the cooler. She assumed it was the cook, who was the only other employee there at the time. When he came in the back door moments later, they both glanced over and saw the misty figure of a woman standing there for a few moments more before vanishing. She has been seen on numerous occasions since.

A woman was shot and killed by a jealous lover in the tavern section of the building on December 22, 1973. Her presence has been felt many times. One night we were taking readings when our compass started fluctuating quite rapidly next to a bar stool, the same spot where she was shot.

Other employees have heard voices from a few feet away resound in the bar and dining rooms. The ghost of a little boy has been seen and heard in the ladies room of the dining area. Another employee, Debbie, has witnessed many of these experiences as well. One day as Eva-Marie was coming to work, she saw Debbie running out of the building. She had been alone in the bar setting up the drink bottles when a voice called out something to her. Frightened and alone, she made a hasty exit.

Former owners, Eugene and Elaine Waterman, tell of coasters flying off the shelves or of full boxes being thrown down the back stairs. Eva-Marie has many times placed the table settings down only to turn her back for a second and find them scattered about the floor. Items fly off the shelves straight through the air at people in the kitchen. Sobbing has been heard by all from the empty dining room and lights always turn on and off

Rear of dining area where the spirit of a woman in nineteenth century dress has been seen sitting in the leftmost booth.

by themselves. Even patrons regularly witness the ghostly phenomenon.

One particular investigation we did proved that there was much activity there. Our EMF meters showed strange fluctuations near an old barber's chair no matter where we moved it. The lights flickered several times when we asked questions in the dining room. I got an EVP recording of a voice that said "WHY?" when I asked if anyone wanted to speak with us. I was sitting in the haunted booth in the back of the dining room at the time.

In the bar, my wife was talking with our friend when her glass shattered into splinters flying as far as three feet into the room. Hers was the only glass among several on the table that exploded. When we had a crystal expert analyze the glass, he stated that the only way that could have happened was if something had struck it from above with great force. These are just some of the multitudes of paranormal events that take place in the old inn. One could write a whole book on the eerie happenings at the Stagecoach Tavern.

The spirits of the tavern are still there and something new happens every day. Present owner Domenic Iocone recently witnessed the ghost of the little boy as he entered the dining room. There near the ladies bathroom was a child standing in front of the door looking at him. The child then walked through the doors of the storage room next to the bathroom. The small storage room was vacant of any living form when he examined it.

Someone recently caught what seems to be the transparent figure of a man carrying a lantern on video. The spirit can be seen walking through the dining room to an old sealed door. Pictures of orbs are common in the historical structure so rich with history and haunts. Domenic Iocone is sure that the ghosts of the tavern are permanently checked in to the antiquated hostelry whether he likes it or not.

The Stagecoach Tavern is located on Route 44 in Chepachet Center. Take Interstate 295 to Exit 7, Greenville. Follow for about nine miles.

# Dark Swamp and H.P. Lovecraft

The legend of Dark Swamp is as thrilling as it gets. Many have avoided the very boundary surrounding the eerie swamp, averting their gaze from the foreboding bog for fear of coming eye to eye with the solitary inhabitant of the evil marsh.

This unusual parcel of land sits amidst several picturesque hills off of Route 94 in the Durfee Hill Management Area. Maps clearly indicate the swamp's location and for good reason. Getting there and traversing the swamp itself is a perilous feat. Great potholes lurk beneath the surface cover and the tree branches form a gnarly snare waiting to catch any person brave or foolish enough to wander into the ever dark and gloomy swamp. Even the sunniest of days cannot permeate the murkiness of the borough.

But even those obstacles are no match for the dreadful dweller of the swamp the Indians have dubbed "IT." Early settlers of the area passed the legend of IT down through the generations. The Indians claimed that IT resided in the muddy bowers of the swamp. IT would appear from the depths when hungry or trespassed upon.

H.P. Lovecraft made several trips to the area in search of the horrible swamp and its creature. Old-timers shared various tales of IT with Lovecraft, who wrote of his fantastic journeys to the outer lands of Glocester in his book, *Selected Letters*.

Here he explained how the local folk abstained from talking much about the area and no one would guide him into the cursed spot. Even the villagers brave enough to build in the area had made their homestead at least a few miles from the swamp.

According to legend, IT rises from the swamp and catches those living creatures foolish enough to trespass upon its domain. The monster snatches them with its great claws and voraciously consumes the unfortunate prey. Hunters stay clear of the land as they know what lurks there. Even the wildlife has migrated to the safer hills of the Connecticut region, beyond the grasp of IT. At night petrifying howls, half human in nature, saturate the air around the swamp.

Because the early settlers avoided much talk about the creature, a lot of history is scarce. We do know Lovecraft never made it to the swamp, but many others, including myself, have negotiated the hazardous territory to get a glimpse of the forbidden bog. It is a good day's adventure so plan accordingly and keep your eyes and ears peeled for strange entities lurk behind the twisted trees of the bog and you do not want to get lost in the sinister basin after what little sunlight seeping through the thick wood has left you in the deep of Dark Swamp.

Dark Swamp is located in Durfee Hill Management Area. Follow directions for the Stagecoach Tavern. Go past the tavern to the light. Bear left at light onto Route 44 West. Follow for five miles. Bear left onto Route 94. Durfee Hill is on your left.

Entrance sign and records building at Acote's Cemetery.

## Acote's Hill Cemetery

Acote's is haunted by the ghost of a peddler who was found murdered on the back stairs of what is now an empty lot on the corner of Route 44 and Route 102. He was taken to the hill entering the village and buried on the western edge of the hill before it was a cemetery because he was not Catholic. This hill was later the scene of the famed Dorr Rebellion of 1842. It has since become a burial ground of all denominations. Many historical cemeteries are relocated to Acote's when progress impedes upon their original locations. This seems to have caused much unrest with the deceased who are dug up from their resting place and buried there. Other witnesses have claimed to see misty figures walking around the old stones during the night and day. It was once the most famous sledding hill for miles around. The winter snow brought people as far as Woodstock, Connecticut, to the giant hills to sled in between the old stones. Now the only activity other than a gravediggers shovel comes from the souls that wander among the obelisks when the time calls for them to make their ethereal rounds. Maybe they were forever disturbed from their eternal sleep by the revelers on the white powder or maybe they are looking for them to come back.

Acote's Hill Cemetery is located on Route 44 in Chepachet. Hours vary and are posted on the gates.

Looking for ghosts from the other side of the wrought iron fence at the old section of Acote's Hill.

## Chepachet Fire Station

Ghostly footsteps on the staircase leading to the second floor have been heard by every person who has ever worked at the station. Foot-steps can be heard coming down the stairs and the door swings open but no visible being is ever there to cause the phenomenon. Occurrences happen at all times of the day and night. I have heard this from everybody I have ever talked to about the building. A lot of functions take place at the fire station but there is no known history behind the haunting. Maybe a few of the ghosts from the Stagecoach Tavern across the street or even Acote's Cemetery down the road have migrated to the fire station.

The fire station is located across from the Stagecoach Tavern on Route 44 in Chepachet.

# Wailing Brook

An Indian man drowned his wife there. Her cries can still be heard through the woods. The actual scene of the crime is lost to legend. If you are in the woods between Elbow Rock Road and Route 94, and hear the weeping of a woman in the woods, map out the area before you run in haste. Wailing Brook is in the woods of Western Glocester between Route 44 and Route 94.

# Jamestown
## The Phantom Dog of Fort Wetherill

We have all at one time or another heard about large black ghostly canines that roam dark roads and remote hills waiting for unsuspecting prey to glimpse their countenances. Once seen, the most evil of fates befalls the observer. They are cursed to die within a short time. They are usually described as large black dogs with glowing red eyes and, in some cases, malevolent snarls.

One such demon dog is known to wander among the ruins of Fort Wetherill in Jamestown. Witnesses have seen the wraith approaching them with its glowing red eyes and white fangs showing through its slavering mouth. Whether or not those who have gazed upon the countenance have suffered for their deed has not been ascertained. The origin of the dog is not clear, but one could trace it back to the time when the English controlled the fort during the American Revolution.

Accounts of the hideous creatures are abundant in Great Britain. One such animal is called the "Moothe Doog" and is known through history to haunt the Castle Peel on the Isle of Man. The very sight of the dog was a harbinger of death. It is documented that a guard once saw the dog in a corridor and was so frightened by the sight he died a few days later, never recovering from his ordeal. Another guard entered an office within the castle and saw the same dog on a chair grimacing at him. The apparition was so horrifying that he succumbed to death moments after his fellow sentinels rushed to investigate the cause of his mortal shrieks. Sentries of the castle now know to avert their eyes when they see the shadow of the phantom in view or they turn and head in the opposite direction for fear of the same fate that has been bestowed upon many of their comrades.

Another such omen of death resides in areas of Norfolk, Essex, and Suffolk along the hills and coastlines of the United Kingdom. He is also known to roam graveyards and country roads. Villagers have for centuries gazed upon the ghostly canine known as "Black Shuck" and never lived long to tell about their encounter with the deadly demon.

When the British took control of the Jamestown hill during the American Revolution, it was known as Dumpling Rock. Colonists had made crude earthwork walls on the rocky hill to control the eastern passageway into

Newport. The British took the area without firing a single shot. They occupied the fort until July 30, 1778, when the French took the harbor. The British fled and destroyed the fort but took it over again a month later. It stayed under their control until October 25, 1779, when they hastily abandoned the fort without explanation. Whether or not the black demon had anything to do with it is not written. You can be sure that an army of men would never divulge such information if it was. This would surely render them as cowards in the laughing faces of the enemy.

The French allies built a better fortress on the rocky defense point called Fort Dumpling or Fort Louis as some referred to it in honor of the king of France. They too soon abandoned the fort unexpectedly.

It was not until 1899, one hundred years later, that the United States Government expanded the fort and put disappearing rifles into cement emplacements that could easily be retracted and hidden from the enemy eye. It was then named Fort Wetherill after Captain Alexander M. Wetherill, who died at San Juan Hill during the Spanish-American War. The fort saw life again until the end of World War I. It was then put on caretaker status until World War II. It saw no military action and was used as a training facility and at one time as a German POW camp for reeducation in the doctrine of Democracy. Once again, it was mysteriously abandoned.

The state acquired fifty-one acres of the property for public use on August 16, 1972. Now the only original dweller of the fort is the black dog that has taken its toll on so many other occupants before as he still haunts the grounds of the decrepit landmark.

Barking has been heard from inside the walls of the fort yet investigations always prove the fort is indeed empty of any living creature. He is also seen walking through walls and sealed doors of the fortress as if they did not exist during his original arrival to the hill. It could be said that the black dog is much like the banshee of Wales whose screams in the night are a sure portent of death to the family who hears them. The only difference is the phantom dog is a wanderer who chooses his victims at random. Those who unexpectedly run into the demon are sure to experience the worst of fates.

So, if you find yourself at Fort Wetherill State Park, perhaps you might want to avoid calling the dark pooch you see in the distance wandering among the ruins. He could just be a neighbor's pet, or his presence could foretell calamity. Do you really want to find out face-to-face?

Jamestown is in the eastern part of Rhode Island and Fort Wetherill is located in the southern tip of the town. Take Interstate Route 95 to Route 4 to Route 1. Take Route138 over the Jamestown Bridge to Cononicus Avenue. Take Walcott Avenue to Fort Wetherill Road. The park is open year round from sunrise to sunset.

# Middletown

## Purgatory Chasm

A view of Purgatory Chasm in Middletown. The haunted crevice is more treacherous than it appears.

Middletown has many legends of Indians that equal most of its neighboring towns. After all the area was Narragansett Indian lands for centuries before the white man came and flooded the area with homes and people. One such place to avoid on a moonlit night is Purgatory Chasm on Tuckerman Road. Roaming the cliffs of the chasm is the headless ghost of an unfortunate squaw.

Legend has it that a local Indian squaw killed a white man and Hobomoko (Native American version of the devil) chopped off her head then threw her off the 160-foot cliffs overlooking 2nd Beach. This was his reward to her for the terrible deed. His footprints still appear in the rocks of the chasm.

A more plausible theory is that an angry mob of friends took justice into their own hands. Either way, witnesses regularly report seeing her headless spirit still roaming the rocky bluffs hundreds of years after her demise.

Middletown is in the eastern tip of the state just north of Newport. Purgatory Chasm is located in the southern tip called Easton Point off Tuckerman Road near the corner of Paradise Avenue. Follow directions for Agincourt Inn but stay on Route 138 past the famous Newport Cliff Walk. Tuckerman Road bears to the right near the water.

## *Agincourt Inn*

Some places harbor spirits from a certain era or event in time. In the case of the Agincourt Inn, spirits of several different periods in history wander amongst the grounds and rooms of the lavish hostel. The original builder of the house is one of the ghosts but there are others, including one apparition that apparently dates back to a time long before the building existed.

In 1856 a wealthy New York businessman by the name of Hamilton Hoppin hired architect Richard Upjohn to build a luxurious summer home on the Newport/ Middletown border. The Hoppin family was very rich. One brother was an illustrator for Mark Twain and a writer himself. Others were doctors, lawyers, and political figures. Hamilton made his fortune presumably manufacturing ammunition and weaponry for the Civil War. Each of the siblings had made their own way in life. It seems some are still making their way in death as well.

The Hoppin family retained the home until the 1890s when the Perry family purchased it. Since then the mansion has changed hands several times. Finally it

The Agincourt Inn is home to a variety of apparitions.

came into the hands of Randy Fabricant and his mother, Selma, in 1994. They made twelve guest rooms upstairs and kept the Victorian décor of the original owners in perfect harmony with the modern necessities of today. Randy told me he named the Agincourt Inn after the Battle of Agincourt fought in October of 1514 between the French and the British. He is an encyclopedia of historical knowledge due to his studies in college. To this day the Fabricant family runs a most welcoming and gracious inn. So welcoming in fact that some of the guests still reside in the walls of the inn.

The ghosts start with simple tricks like opening and closing doors or moving objects around the inn. Items placed in one area will disappear in front of your eyes and be found somewhere else in the house. A guest saw a perfume bottle inexplicably slide across a dresser in her room. A psychic went into the house and verified without prior knowledge that a fight once took place in that room and a perfume bottle was thrown and smashed against the wall. The basement seems to harbor a collection of spirits and with good reason. It was used as a hiding place for slaves during the Underground Railroad and the tunnels and rooms now echo with the sounds of the unfortunate who got ill and died on their way to freedom. According to Randy, this seems to be the scariest part of the whole house.

Randy's mother had quite an alarming experience once in the house as well. Selma Fabricant went to bed early one night. She was suddenly awoken by a noise. When she opened her eyes she saw an Indian in full war paint at the foot of her bed. He had a tomahawk in his hand. She blinked quickly to make sure she was awake and the figure vanished into the night air. What was the phantom of a Narragansett Indian doing in a nineteenth century home? When Randy did some research, he found out the house was built on an old Indian path that led to an estuary. He concluded that the specter was walking down the path that existed during his lifetime.

Randy did a lot more digging into the history of his inn and found a portrait of Hamilton's brother, Thomas Hoppin. They brought the painting home and put it in the ballroom that night for future hanging. The next morning the Fabricants noticed that every clock in the inn had been turned back exactly one hour. "I can't explain that one," Randy admitted with a puzzled snigger.

One evening a group of diners got more than the elegant cuisine served at the stylish inn. As they sat at the dining room table, the candles began to flicker and the dogs began to bark. Then a glass on the table moved. In the next frightful moment, there were the ghosts of Hamilton Hoppin and his brother, Thomas, standing in front of the stunned guests holding an ethereal conversation with each other. According to witnesses, the two spirits went back and forth, mingling with the help as if the world of the living was not there. They dematerialized as the conversation faded into thin air as well.

Another apparition seen once a year at the inn is that of a phantom automobile that drives up Miantonomi Avenue and pulls into the driveway of the Agincourt. The ghost car pulls up to the door then disappears. The story behind it is that of a doctor and his wife who were residing at the mansion between owners in the very early 1900s. The doctor was reprehensible in both practice and marriage. He was having affairs with many of the woman in town. It was no secret to his wife, who was well aware of his evil doings. He also had one of the first "horseless" carriages in the town. One day as he drove up the driveway towards the house, he was shot and killed. His wife was put on trial for the murder but was acquitted. It is said that the trial rivaled that of the famous Lizzie Borden several years before. It is that very early automobile seen once a year pulling up the driveway then vanishing as the infamous doctor is eternally trying to make it home.

Many guests still see and hear these spirits as well as one of a woman seen in one of the guest rooms floating over the bed. Randy told me that the New Year brought another strange incident into the growing collection of stories about entities in the manor. A week before I had talked to him, a woman staying at the inn was walking towards the stairs when she saw an old gentleman sitting on the porch in what looked like nineteenth century attire. The seemingly living man looked over at the woman and vanished right in front of her.

Randy says that some guests are excited to be in a place that is so haunted and others do not want to know anything about the ghosts. Many have checked into the inn as skeptics and came out with a new outlook on the afterlife.

Agincourt Inn is located at 120 Miantonomi Avenue. Take Interstate Route 95 to Route 4 to Route 1. Take Route 138 East. Miantonomi Avenue crosses Route 138 at the Newport/Middletown border.

# Garden of Angels

This is an area of the Newport Memorial Park cemetery where about two-dozen infants have been interred over the last fifty years. At midnight or when the moon is full, one can hear the babies crying in the most ghostlike weep. Paranormal investigator Paul Eno is among the many who have heard the spectral whines.

The cemetery is located on Memorial Boulevard between Newport and Middletown.

# Narragansett
## Old Wedderburn Mansion

Japheth Wedderburn was a successful sea captain who lived in a four-story mansion by the shores of the Narragansett Bay. His only companion when at home was his servant Huldy Craddock who cared for the immense home when the captain was away at sea.

One day the captain returned to his mansion from a trip overseas with a new bride by the name of Donna Mercedes. The local residents often saw the petite young Spanish woman in her black lace mantilla dress with a tortoise shell comb for her hair staring out the windows of the manor with an acute expression of sorrow on her face. It must have been terribly lonely for a girl who did not speak English and was married to a possessive, jealous man of the sea.

Good lady Craddock tried to accommodate her but she missed her family back in the homeland and wanted desperately to return there. When Captain Wedderburn returned form a journey, it is said he agreed to sail his bride back to her own country and all would go back to the way it once was.

Two years later he returned from the long voyage telling all the townsfolk that she was again living with her family. This would have been the end of the story, except people of the town began to see the diminutive figure of a woman pacing to and fro in the windows of the great hall and heard sobbing that they had come to recognize as that of Donna Mercedes herself.

Even after the death of Japheth Wedderburn, the new owners of the house heard the sobbing of a woman and witnessed her apparition on the third floor overlooking the ocean. Every new family in turn would live with the mournful ghost of Donna Mercedes until 1925 when renovations were being done in the house. As they tore up the hearthstone in the library, they noticed a small wooden coffin. When they pried it open, to their astonishment, they found the skeleton of a woman in a tattered and rotted black lace mantilla. At the top of her skull was a great tortoise shell comb.

Some say she was killed by her husband, who could not stand to let her go, while others believe she was murdered by the housekeeper, who may have fallen for the sea captain herself and wanted her out of the way. When he found out, they buried her to avoid any confrontation with the law. The truth went to the grave many years ago. Apparently so did the house.

The mansion was supposedly located on Front Street in Narragansett. No such road exists in the state maps. I have found the ruins of a mansion off of Ocean Drive. Could Ocean Drive have once been called Front Street? No historical records indicate either way. If you hear cries coming from the remains of an old mansion on a moonlit night you might be in the right place. Whether it is the sobbing of Donna Mercedes or not, let's let you, the reader, decide.

# New Shoreham
# (Block Island)
## The Spring House Hotel's
## Eternal Chambermaid

Some people take their jobs seriously. So seriously in this case that a certain chambermaid has stayed on almost one hundred years after her death. The Spring House Hotel is located on a hill overlooking the ferry landing on Block Island. Block Island is a small coastal land mass set in Narragansett Bay between the southern tip of Rhode Island and Long Island, New York. It is actually a part of the State of Rhode Island, which is why it is included in this book.

My best friend's aunt, Beatrice Cyr, owns the Ocean View Hotel out on the island and my friend spent many summers there. He had a lot of stories to share about the haunted places as well as other interesting facts.

The island itself was becoming a Mecca for the elite in the nineteenth century. Tourists flocked to the private island for summer vacations and it was only a matter of time before great hotels would replace run down cottages. The Spring House Hotel was built in 1852 to accommodate the upper crust of society. Business boomed for Block Island's first hotel and it was expanded to forty-nine rooms by 1870. Many of the island's local inhabitants found work at the grand hotel. One such woman, who was known as "Clossie," took the position of head chambermaid before the turn of the twentieth century.

She held her position well and made sure it was known who was the boss. Her checking and rechecking of the subordinate's toils was constant and meticulous. Not as much as a wrinkle was allowed in the turning of the sheets. Every mantle, lamp, and table had to be spotless upon the guest's checking in.

Her death around 1920 did not stop her from keeping future chambermaids in line. Even now the employees are compelled to live up to her precise standards. Or else!

Room M13 seems to house her spirit most actively. Fans have turned on in the room suddenly and guests have complained of the bed rattling. A child once saw an old woman in the room late at night after the lights were out. When the parents investigated, there was no one.

Hotel managers have heard voices from empty rooms in the main building, proving that "Clossie" makes her rounds there as well. One of the employees had just finished cleaning up the third floor and securing each room for the winter when she heard a noise. When she looked back, she found, to her shock, all the doors on the floor wide open.

Another spirit resides in room 315 as well. A chambermaid who was cleaning the bathroom saw the ghost of a man in old-fashioned attire when she glanced into the mirror. The specter was sitting on the bed. When she turned towards him, he was gone.

The haunted hotel still gets an enormous amount of guests each summer and "Clossie" is still there to make sure their stays are as grand as they were when she was there in more than just spirit if you know what I mean.

Block Island can be reached by ferry from Galilee near Point Judith. Take Interstate Route 95 to Route 4. Route 4 merges with Route 1. Take Narragansett exit, Route 108 to Sand Hill Cove Road. A schedule is available from Interstate Navigation Company, (203) 442-7891.

# The Southeast Light

Lighthouses always seem to have an air of mystery to them. These great beacons of luminous warning to the helpless seafarers are ripe with legends and tales of the seas. In this case they are the accounts of a bona fide haunted lighthouse.

Looming over the Mohegan Bluffs stands the island's Southeast Lighthouse. The bluff's rocky edifice rises two hundred feet above the crashing waves and the sixty-seven foot high lighthouse was put into operation in 1875 to warn mariners of the abrupt impending doom that towers into the heavens from the sea. The light is the largest reflecting light on the Eastern Seaboard, thus securing its place in the National Historical Register. It has also secured its places among the registers and books of the paranormal as being one of the most haunted lighthouses in the nation.

The ghost of the lighthouse is a woman who was named Maggie Brown. She was the wife of one of the first light keepers. Whether he was driven mad from desolation or by her is not known. What is known is that he threw her down the long spiral staircase of the lantern room, ending her physical existence, but not her spectral one.

Although he claimed it was suicide, he was convicted of murder and paid for his deed. He is long gone but she has stayed on to seek vengeance on all men who dare enter the structure. Objects can be seen moving about and furniture shakes and rattles. Even the caretaker's bed has been literally moved while he was in it. Doors open and slam shut by an unseen force. A light keeper was even chased out of the beaconed domicile one night by the angry ghost. She then locked the door, leaving him half dressed in the night until another Coast Guardsman arrived to unlock the door.

Food flying in the kitchen and dishes breaking on their own is not an uncommon occurrence. She has been seen floating up and down the stairs she was thrown down and caretakers as well as tour guides have heard her shrieks echo through the massive tower at all hours.

An anonymous tour guide who was afraid to admit he believed in the paranormal despite his experiences recounted the facts to me. I had won his trust with my knowledge and love for the supernatural realm. He even let me take some readings and recordings but nothing peculiar was going on at that time. A caretaker on the scene was the opposite. He believed in the stories, sightings, and experiences he had with the haunted lighthouse. He told me once he was outside with another guide and heard a shrill scream. When they ran to the building, they found the door locked. A spare key was procured and upon getting the door unlocked, it slammed shut again. This time it was accompanied by the crashing of dishes on the floor.

The hexed lighthouse was moved inland two hundred and forty five feet from its previous location due to the heavy erosion of the bluffs. The spirit diligently went with it in her ghostly mission to wreak havoc upon every male who enters the building on either a tour or tour of duty.

# The Palatine Light

Although the story of the Palatine Light has been told many times over, I feel I must include it here as well. Maybe this account will shed some light on the story as it is the most accurate to date. It is by far the most famous of Block Island's ghosts. Or, should I say ghost ships.

The true name of the ship was called the Princess Augusta. It was a three-mast brigantine tall ship that sailed out of Rotterdam, Holland, around 1732 filled with 340 Palatines coming to Philadelphia for a better life. Bad luck beset the ship from the start.

The water supply on board turned out to be contaminated. This left many sick and a lot of the passengers and crew died from the poisoned water. One of the first to die was George Long, Captain of the Princess Augusta. This left First Mate Andrew Brook in charge. He was obviously not suited for the job as the situation aboard the vessel began to deteriorate.

With 250 passengers and several crewmembers already dead, the crew was on the verge of mutiny. It is rumored that the crew stole money and food from the passengers and that they sold food for excessive amounts of money to the starving pilgrims. Those who could not pay the price for the meager rations starved to death. No one knows for sure but they were lost and the storms were bashing the ship to pieces. Bitter cold snow was also taking its toll on the surviving throng. As the storm worsened, all seemed lost when a man in the crow's nest spotted a signal fire in the distance. As the ship sped towards the light there was a terrible crushing sound that shook the boat. The Princess Augusta had hit some rocks just below the surface of the water. The ship was flooding fast.

Some tried to swim for shore, some clung to the crumbling vessel, and many drowned in the storm and raging sea. The survivors saw lanterns and torches coming down the hill and were relieved that the townspeople were coming to their rescue. This relief was short lived when they realized that the lights were those of "wreckers" who made a living out of luring ships to a false safety then plundering the wreckage for any valuables they could find.

The wreckers took all they could and retreated back into the hills. Other villagers from New Shoreham came down and brought the survivors to safety. The sinking ship was then set afire. Records do not indicate if the plunderers burned the ship or the villagers for fear of being a safety hazard for future navigation in the area. The burning ship somehow wrenched free from the rocks and drifted out to sea where it eventually sank. Folklore relates that one crazy woman remained on the ship after it was set on fire and went out to sea with the burning boat. It is said her screams of agony could be heard from shore as the ship went to its watery grave with her aboard.

Whatever the case may be, The Princess Augusta appeared two years later on the horizon. At first no one thought anything about the approaching brigantine. As it came rapidly closer they became alarmed at the fact that the tall ship was racing towards shore under full sail with no one at the helm. Just before it hit the shore it burst into flames and vanished. That night a terrible storm followed. So fierce was the wind and rain that it sent three ships in the Block Island Harbor to the bottom of the ocean.

A year later, the same ship was spotted racing towards the shore only to burst into flames and disappear in front of many terrified witnesses. People began to wonder if the Princess Augusta was returning to seek revenge on the people who caused her untimely demise on the high seas. Almost every year since, the phantom ship has been spotted burning off the shore of Block Island, followed by a horrific storm. In 1865, John

Greenleaf Whittier penned a famous poem about the apparition called "The Palatine," thus forging much folklore into the true horror the passengers and crew experienced on their journey into eternity.

To this day the ship is still seen in the waters off the Block Island shores. Woe to the seasoned sailor who sees the burning ship racing towards shore and does not turn around for dry land. For he will certainly be driven to the bottom of the sea.

See above for directions to the island.

# Newport
## Belcourt Castle

Newport has always been known as the playground of the rich and famous. The mansions are breathtaking in their wealth and splendor. The views along Ocean Drive and the famous Cliff Walk are equally wondrous. No wonder so many people flock to this tourist location each year. It is also understandable why so many have never left. Even after they are long dead.

Belcourt Castle is a perfect example of a mansion found in Newport — lavish, extravagant, and haunted. The manor is home to many spirits according to Donald and Harley Tinney. The Tinney family own the house and give tours regularly. Specters have been seen in the bedrooms, entering the bathroom, and on the stairs to name just a few places.

Belcourt Castle's origins are as opulent as Newport's finest can boast. It was designed by Richard Morris Hunt for Oliver Hazard Perry Belmont

Belcourt Castle.

and built in 1894. Hunt's other designs include the base of the Statue of Liberty, the Vanderbuilt homes, and the United States Capitol. The building was fashioned after Louis XIII's hunting lodge in Versailles, France. It was also made so that Mr. Belmont could actually drive his carriage into the mansion. Thomas Edison designed the indirect lighting which graces the manor to this day. The stained glass window collection is the largest of its kind in the country and dates as far back as the thirteenth century.

The sixty-room house was completed in 1894 for a sum of three million dollars. Mr. Belmont did not enjoy his beloved creation for too long. He died in 1908 at the age of fifty. His wife retained the house until her death in 1938. The remaining heirs to the Belmont family sold the property in 1940. It remained unoccupied and deteriorated rapidly until the Tinney family bought it in 1956 for a mere twenty-five thousand dollars. They renovated the mansion back to its original splendor, then filled it with the family heirlooms and antiques it displays at present.

Harley and Donald Tinney moved into the manor shortly after they were married in 1960. The first few months were quiet, but then one night Harley was rustled from her sleep by a noise. There at the foot of the bed was the figure of a man holding onto the canopy post. She tried to rouse Donald but he was too deep into his sleep to make any fuss. She thought at first they were going to be robbed. Then the man turned around and slowly walked through the wall on the other side of the room.

A few years later they were waiting for his parents to come down the great ballroom staircase as they were going to Providence for the day. At that moment Donald and Harley both saw an old man they thought to be his father enter the ladies room in the ballroom. They waited for a long time until his Aunt Nellie came in and told them that his parents had been waiting in the car for them for fifteen minutes. Donald went to check the bathroom. He came out with a strange look on his face. The bathroom was empty. No one could have come out without being seen.

After that incident they began to see the ghost of a monk between the ballroom and the chapel. They have a wooden statue of a monk that Harley had placed near the grand staircase. Witnesses spotted the phantom monk on the stairs for some time. One night a tour guide was telling a group about the statue when the throng became quite unnerved by the apparition of the monk that appeared behind her. Another woman on a tour asked who the priest was setting up the altar in the chapel. Harley told the woman there is no priest on the premises but she insisted she watched a man of the cloth preparing for mass. A psychic told Mrs. Tinney that the statue wanted to be put in the chapel or it would never be at peace. She did just that and the sightings of the phantom monk now remain isolated to that room.

There are two gothic salt chairs of past royalty in the vaulted ballroom. These chairs had backs on them when most chairs of the castle did not. Whatever happened in these chairs is not known but they emit a furious form of energy. Tourists of the manor have touched the chairs and have felt the blood leave their hands. One woman was supposedly thrown into the center of the room when she tried to sit in one of the chairs. Since then the chairs have been roped off for safety. No one can explain the violent force the chairs contain except that whoever met their end in them is eternally angry.

The spirit of the monk and the chairs pale in comparison to the spine-chilling presence that haunts one of the eight suits of armor that terrorize the occupants and visitors of the house. The suit of armor in question was purchased by the Tinney family then set up in front of the ballroom with the other suits. One night as Harley was getting sugar from the main wing, she noticed the stained glass lights were on. As she approached the ballroom she heard a blood-curdling scream. At first she thought it was Kevin Tinney, the adopted son of her mother-in-law, Ruth, and his friend who were having dinner on the third floor, playing a bad joke on her. She turned off the lights and went back to her original quest. She turned back and the lights were on again. This time there was a scream even more terrifying than the first. Scared stiff she turned the lights off again. The third and most hideous scream made her break for the door. Once on the other side of the door she called to the third floor, where no one had moved all night. She coaxed Donald to take the rottweilers and have a look. When the dogs came to the door of the main building they would not budge. Donald could not even drag the fearsome creatures past the threshold.

Tour guide Virginia Smith was locking up for the evening when she heard a guttural moan coming from the direction of the armor. The moan turned into a frightening shriek that stopped her dead in her tracks. She too left the building in haste. Since then she has heard the scream several times. They have also witnessed the armor's right arm raise just before the scream is heard. When they got the armor, they noticed that there was a hole in the back of the helmet that resembled a chop from a battleaxe. They seem to think that whoever was in the armor when he was hit died in the suit and is very unhappy about his fate. The hole was fixed but the armor still wails with unearthly screams, recapturing the warrior's gruesome final moments in battle.

The mansion is located at 657 Bellevue Avenue. Take Interstate 95 to Route 4, to Route1. Take Route 138 East over the Jamestown Bridge then the Pell Bridge. Follow Route 138 to Bellevue Avenue. Go south on Bellevue Avenue. Tours run from noon to five, Wednesday to Monday. Ghost tours run on Wednesdays and Thursdays at 5:00 PM.

# Brenton Point

If you were unaware of the bizarre story associated with Brenton Point, you would be left scratching your head, wondering why a wealthy family would abandon such beautiful ocean front property. The fact that it is haunted adds to the mystery of this cursed ground.

Brenton Point is named after William Brenton, an early settler who farmed the area in question during the seventeenth century. Theodore M. Davis acquired the land in 1876 and erected "The Reef." This was a large shingled mansion with high chimneys and large windows for viewing the bay. He was a man of wealth. Not only was he a lawyer, he was also

Picture of the "Reef" as it looked before the tragic fire. The postcard is on public display in the tourist information center. *Courtesy of the RI DEM Division of Parks and Recreation.*

one of the most famous Egyptologists of his time. It is the latter profession that would bring a dark cloud upon his land that to this day seems to still linger among the trees of the park.

Mr. Davis, you see, went on two very special expeditions. Both were in Egypt's Valley of the Kings, where he led the expedition that found King Tut's father and accompanied others in search for the child-king himself. As everyone knows, great curses were to befall those who desecrated the tombs of the ancient pharaohs. As you read on, you can see why many think the curse befell the Davis family.

When Theodore Davis built the manor, he also built great gardens as gardening was one of his fancies. He had the finest gardens in all of Newport at one time. No less a sight was his beautiful stable built out of stone to be both fashionable and fireproof. The tower had a four-faced clock and musical chimes. The stables held a dozen hands, horses, carriages, and later motorcars. The gardener's building and servants' quarters were also the laundry room and heating plant for the main house. A windmill was built on the estate for pumping water to all the buildings. Because of his many important archeological discoveries in the Valley of the Kings, the main house contained the finest private collection of Egyptian antiquities in the country — all spoils of his digs at the hallowed tombs.

The curse struck early when the windmill caught fire in a storm and burned to the ground. Very shortly after, the stables were struck with the same fate. With no windmill to pump the water, the damaged stables and windmill were rebuilt using better material. The windmill was made of stone and the stables used steel reinforcements to keep them from collapsing. Mr. Davis never had absolute peace at his estate he bought with the wealth of the Egyptian kings.

Theodore Davis died in 1910, followed by his wife in 1915. The estate was abandoned until 1923 when Milton J. Budlong, an automobile sale mogul, purchased the cursed manor. The Budlongs soon found themselves in an immense divorce suit and the house and great expanse of property stood once again abandoned. Even his children shied from the home for unknown reasons. When Mr. Budlong died in 1941, the United States Army commandeered the property as a coastal defense point and even put up a gun turret overlooking the Brenton Point Reef. The remains of the turret still stand in the field in front of the servants' quarters that now serve as the park administration building. In 1946, the land was given back to the Budlong family but no one would live in the mansion. It is unclear why, as they never disclosed their personal reasons to anybody about the strange happenings within the house. We do know that the incredible piece of land stood vacant for many years. The family did not want the property.

In July of 1960, a great fire destroyed the decaying mansion that had to be torn down in 1963 because it was a public safety hazard. In 1969 the State took over the abandoned property at the will of the family and began making it into the public park it is today.

Since then, scores of visitors have experienced why the families of the estate may not have wanted to live on the unholy grounds. There are bizarre noises in the gardens that seemingly emanate from nowhere. Many people have been taken aback at the sound of horses trotting down the paths, only to see nothing when they turn or move out of the way to let the ethereal steeds pass. Phantom conversations are heard near the windmill and stables on the calmest of days and voices lurk around the gnarled trees in the great gardens. The trees themselves harbor negative energy that seems to create a foreboding atmosphere in the vicinity where they sit most menacing along the edge of the woods.

Park Rangers have actually admitted that they would not venture into the grounds alone after the sun has set for fear of what they have witnessed in the daylight hours.

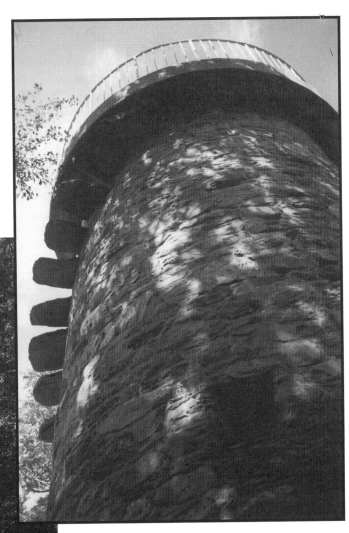

Looking up at the windmill once used to draw water for the estate.

Remains of the great stable at Brenton Point State Park.

A group of investigators got permission to do paranormal research in the park after dark. The rangers were too reluctant to accompany them. They got some EVP recordings of ghost voices and heavy EMF readings around the trees. EVP is short for Electronic Voice Phenomena and EMF is short for Electro-Magnetic Frequency. EVP recordings have been instrumental in the proof of paranormal activity as have EMF readings. When activity is present, EMF readings become higher than normal. According to their reports, the place is definitely alive with the spirits of what once was.

Whether it was the curse of the kings or the ghosts of the past keeping the owners away who might now haunt the grounds themselves we will never know. We do know that Brenton Point State Park holds a host of entities that do not abide by the rules of the park, which is supposed to be vacated by sunset.

Brenton Point is located on Ocean Drive at the Southwest tip of Newport. Follow directions above to Newport. Ocean Drive is clearly marked.

# La Petite Auberge
# French Restaurant

This bistro of fine food was once a colonial home turned restaurant. It still boasts the ancient fireplaces and remnants of early American life, including previous owners who have yet to leave the building.

A cook passing an upstairs room after the restaurant had been locked up noticed a man dressed in ancient attire seated at a table. When she confronted him about his being there after business hours, he vanished before her eyes. The owner's wife once turned around and saw the distinct form of a ghost sitting behind her. Silverware often rattles at random on the tables. The kitchen doors have opened and closed by themselves when no one was around but the owner or his wife.

Guests and patrons of the restaurant often encounter the spirit of the house. The A&E Channel did a TV special on ghosts and included this restaurant in the roster of haunts. Now it is famous for more than just exceptionally delicious food.

The restaurant is located at 19 Charles Street. Take Thames Street to Washington Street to Charles Street. Charles Street is near the Gateway Information Center when you enter Newport.

Astors Beechwood Mansion.

Doors to the two bedrooms where a phantom woman in yellow dress has been seen entering.

## Astors Beechwood Mansion

Mansions always hold the creepy sounds of ghostly turmoil and eerie shadows that dart from one edge of your eye to the empty corners of the room. The Beechwood mansion is no exception. This manor has valid reason to harbor the presence of another realm.

The mansion was built in 1851 for a New York merchant named Daniel Parrish by architects Andrew Jackson Downing and Calvert Vaux. William Blackhouse Astor Jr. purchased the mansion in 1881. He was the grandson of John Jacob Astor, who is the fourth wealthiest man in American history. John Jacob Astor's business deals in the fur trade and real estate made the family wealthy beyond measure.

The Astors spent an extra two million dollars decorating the home so as to impress and

Closet where a member of the theatre group heard the ghostly sighs as she was tidying up.

make welcome the elite society of friends they entertained in the luxurious summer home. Eight weeks out of the year the mansion's walls rang with merriment and mirth among the best of the best. The grandest of all was the final summer ball where "The Mrs. Astor" became hostess unmatched.

With the passing of Mr. Astor, social life at the mansion came to a halt. Caroline Schermerhorn-Astor passed away in 1908. The house was left to their son, John Jacob Astor IV. After the death of his mother, John Jacob Astor IV divorced his wife, Ava Lowell Willing. About this time in the history of the Astor manor, things begin to turn.

In 1911, a telephone repairman was working in the basement when he came in contact with some high voltage wiring. The result was fatal. It is the only known death in the house that is on record. The young man's mother sued Mr. Astor for a hefty sum of his inheritance. That same year, he married Madeleine Talmadge, a woman much younger than he was. They both set off for Europe after a magnificent wedding held in the ballroom of the Beechwood. The extensive honeymoon lasted until April of 1912 when they left London to return home to Newport via New York. The ship they boarded was the RMS *Titanic*.

Madeleine, who was five months pregnant, survived the tragedy but the wealthiest man on the ship did not. As history would play out, so would the ghosts of the Beechwood survive.

The Beechwood is presently open for tours. The tours take on different themes such as the roaring twenties, or murder-mystery tours. All are interactive so you can experience the gilded age or the golden age up close and personal. More up close and personal are the spirits also residing in the Beechwood. Patrick Grimes, Production Manager of the Astor's Beechwood Theatre Company, told me that there are many unusual occurrences that take place in the building.

One notable haunting in particular is of a young woman in a maid's uniform who has been seen in various parts of the house. It is said that she committed suicide in the house after being spurned by a lover. Although the ghost is real, the story does not have any documentation to prove it.

Louis Seymour, of the Beechwood Theatre Company, recounted some experienced he had concerning a woman in a yellow ball gown. The cast of the theatre company reside on the third floor where it is set up like a giant apartment. One day he was watching television with fellow cast member Jen Leibowitz. A little off to the side of their vision came a woman in a yellow gown. Both of them knew that Morgan, who was another part of the crew, had a yellow gown and wore it on occasion, sometimes even when cleaning the house. The figure went towards two corner doors where two bedrooms are located. A few moments later the phone rang. It was a call for Morgan. Jen got off the couch to get her but there was no one in either of the rooms. They had seen her go towards the two doors just off to the left of the parlor. Later, Morgan came in from an appointment she had in Warwick and swore that she was never there until that instant.

A most recent sighting of the woman in yellow was at the end of 2004. Casey Kogut's roommate, Mary, also has a yellow period dress she sometimes wears for occasions. One day while she was upstairs she saw "Mary" in her yellow dress walk into their room. She went into the room to chat with her but the room was completely empty. The way the third floor is designed resembles a studio apartment with bedrooms off of the main large room so no one can sneak by someone who might be in the large room without being seen. Another member of the troupe by the name of Peg Kiernan was alone in Mrs. Astor's dressing room putting clothes in the closet when she was shaken by the sound of a heavy, disgusted sigh right behind her. She was taken aback by it so much she comforted the ghost by saying she was just putting some items away and would be out of her room in a moment. Peg was convinced it was Mrs. Astor showing her disapproval of her being in the room.

In January of 2005, a cast member by the name of C.C. was alone downstairs in the manor closing up for the evening. Her usual routine was to close all the doors to the rooms before retreating to her upstairs quarters. As she started up the stairs she noticed a door was open. She was sure she had just closed it. When she went to inspect the situation, she found several doors to the rooms suddenly open and all the doors inside the rooms as well.

Additionally, candles blow out by themselves when there is no wind. Many of the cast claim to have seen eerie images and have heard very uncanny noises around them. Louis attributes some of these occurrences to the house being old and settling or the size of the rooms casting long shadows on the walls. They cannot explain the sighs of disgust nor can they rationally explain the lady in yellow. Several of cast members have witnessed her. Two people at the same time attest to her walking by them.

Next time you are in Newport you must book a slot with the Beechwood Theatre Company. The tours and special shows are well worth your time. You might even meet an extra that is not cast in the script.

The mansion is located at 580 Bellevue Avenue. Follow directions above or call (401) 846-3772 for reservations and schedules.

# Black Duck Inn

The Black Duck was originally a rum-running vessel that smuggled liquor into Newport Harbor in 1929 during Prohibition. The Coast Guard was furious over the unlawful excursions yet the wealthy locals found it to be a comfort in this "dry time" of the twentieth century. The Coast Guard eventually caught up with the Black Duck on a foggy night and open fired upon its decks, killing three out of the four crewmen in the process. The

The Black Duck Inn.

unwarranted action created a mob in the streets and no Coast Guardsman was safe from being attacked. This incident brought national attention to the area and even the White House had to deal with the situation. The surviving rum smuggler went to trial but was acquitted by his peers.

The present Black Duck is a bed and breakfast that sits on Pelham Street above Newport Harbor. The house was built in 1898 as a duplex but was later converted into an inn. It stood vacant for two years before Mary Rolando purchased it in 1994. She renovated the decaying structure into the charming lodge that sits most welcoming among the other historic homes on Pelham Street. At first gaze you get the immediate impulse to enter the quaint eightguestroom hostel. Once inside you will find it hard to leave. Don't worry, it seems a few spirits feel the same way as well.

The phantoms of the manor mostly play with lights and deadbolts. The unseen guests also like to turn radios on. One time all the alarm clocks in the guest rooms went off at the same time. Mary related to me that guests have told her they heard talking in the rooms next to them when the doors were open and the rooms were visibly empty. Mary even heard the ghostly voices before Christmas while tidying up a room. She was alone in the house when suddenly she heard a low mumbling voice near her. She said, "It was so low at first, I was wondering if I was actually hearing what I thought I was." The voice got a little louder than faded into space.

Another common occurrence is that of ghostly footsteps in the rooms when she is sure they are empty. The footsteps happen at all hours of the day and night. They are the same each time so she knows the clopping of guests and the unearthly sound of her ghost walking about the building. Mary does not know who the ghosts are. She only knows that they are very friendly and have never harmed or frightened anybody. There is always something interesting from the night before to talk about at breakfast that includes a different delicious hot entree each day for you to enjoy and maybe share with your friendly caretaker. Either the one you can see or the one you can't.

The inn is located at 29 Pelham Street across from the famous Bannister Wharf on America's Cup Avenue. See above for directions. (401) 841-5548.

# America's Oldest Ghosts

One of the oldest taverns in America sits in downtown Newport. The building was constructed in 1673 as a private residence by Francis Brinley but became a tavern in 1687 when William Mayes Sr. bought the parcel. Mayes son was an infamous pirate. When he settled in Newport, he took over as innkeeper. Later he handed operation of the tavern to his sister, Mary Mayes Nichols. The tavern stayed in the Nichols family for two hundred years. In 1901 it was sold and became a boarding house. In 1954 the Preservation Society acquired the aging structure and renovated it. It then reopened as a restaurant and tavern in 1957. It has been that since. The tavern looks like it did back in the seventeenth century. The ghosts seem to like it that way as well.

Anita Rafael is curator of the tavern and hosts a walking tour of Newport. During the Halloween season, Anita does ghost tours as well. She has told historians Christopher Martin and Dan Hillman of the many encounters with the spirits of the tavern. In fact almost every employee has a story to tell. One night while closing up, two employees heard footsteps in the room. They both grabbed something to protect themselves as they started up the stairs. When they met in the middle of the stairs the footsteps were gone. They then realized they were alone in the building the whole time.

The ghosts like to make their presence known in other ways as well. They tap people on the shoulder, they tell the staff to lock up, and the spirits have even appeared to customers. A little boy once saw a man in old clothing. This is not so surprising as many of the staff have seen the colonial ghost as well. A woman claimed that a ghost was bothering her one night at dinner. So much so, that she and her companion had to take their food to go.

Who could the man in the old clothes be? Around 1720 two men arrived at the tavern and took lodging there. Mary Nichols and her husband, Robert, gave them a room to share. The next morning neither of the men came downstairs for breakfast. When Mary and her servant went upstairs to check on the men, they found one man dead in the room and the other was gone. The man had not been murdered. There was no sign of a struggle. They feared he may have died from a sudden illness and buried him hastily in a pauper's grave. At the time diseases such as smallpox or tuberculosis were highly contagious and very deadly. The identity of the man was never discovered. It could be the ghost of the unknown traveler who now haunts the tavern looking for someone to identify him or solve the mystery of his death.

The area that is the most haunted is a room behind the large fireplace. The right-hand side of the fireplace in that room is

The White Horse Tavern. Home to some of America's oldest ghosts.

where the ghost is usually seen. Ghost hunters and legend trippers have gone to the tavern and come out with a story to tell. Reports of spirit encounters are too numerous to remember, according to Anita Rafael.

Come for dinner and experience the fine cuisine, then partake in a spirit or two after. They do have plenty to go around.

Follow the directions above for Newport. Take America's Cup Ave. Take a left onto Marlborough Street. Tavern is at the corner of Marlborough and Farewell Streets. For reservations and tour information, call (401) 849-3600.

# North Kingstown
## Devil's Foot Rock

The ghost of Peter Rugg is legendary throughout New England. His eternally wandering spirit has been spotted from Newburyport, Maine, to Hartford, Connecticut, but it is in North Kingstown, Rhode Island, where the only physical proof of his phantom journey is set in stone.

Our story begins in 1770 when Boston native Peter Rugg set out on a business trip to Concord, Massachusetts. On such a pleasant day he saw no reason to deny his daughter, Jenny, who was ten years old, a chance to go with him on the day trip. All went well for the ride up, but a terrible storm brewed in the sky and unleashed its wrath upon the weary returning travelers. So much so that Peter Rugg and his daughter sought shelter at Tom Cutter's home to wait out the storm. When he realized the storm was not going to let up he became determined to get home despite the pleadings of his friend and the condition of his daughter. Rugg swore at that moment he would see his home by the God or the devil that night or he will never see home again.

Peter Rugg never made it home. Family, friends, and neighbors searched for months but not a trace of the carriage or its occupants were ever found. It wasn't until Spring the following year that residents of Middle Street in Boston were roused from their slumber in the wee hours of the morning by the clomping of hooves on the cobblestone street. There in the misty street was the glowing nightshade of a phantom chaise drawn by a mammoth horse with two figures in it. They knew it was Peter Rugg and his daughter but they also knew he was no longer among the living. Thomas Felt shuddered in terror of the unearthly sight.

Other encounters of the ghostly carriage ensued throughout the region. Adonariah Adams was overtaken by the specter while delivering mail. Rugg's coach came at him so fast his horses jumped from the road and wrecked his carriage. Rugg's horse, a roman-nosed bay had burning red eyes and the smell of brimstone. He swore it was the devil's shade of Peter Rugg that day.

A toll booth operator who had many run-ins with the ghost even threw his stool at the passing apparition one evening in disgust. The stool went through the horse and hit the guardrail on the other side of the road. Many travelers would encounter the spirit of Rugg, who would stop and

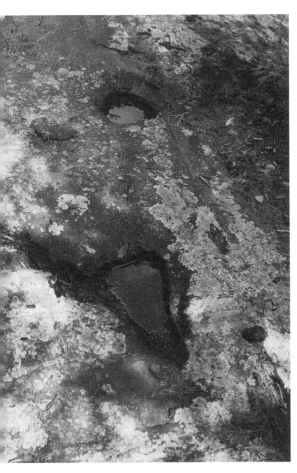

ask directions to Boston then ride off at a furious clip. Shortly after, a terrible storm would overtake the unsuspecting sojourners. Of all the witnesses who swore they saw Peter Rugg's ghoulish carriage, none was more reliable than Reverend Samuel Nickles of Providence.

Reverend Nickles was returning to Providence from the village of Wickford when he and his old nearsighted nag, Romeo, were caught in a dreadful storm. The Reverend hunched his coat over his head and bade his trusty steed to push onward towards home. As they entered a narrow passage between a great rock and a ledge, the sound of thunder-

Hoof prints left in rock by Peter Rugg's devil horse.

Hoof prints run all the way up the rock.

ous hooves filled his frightened ears. He looked up and saw a wagon with a man desperately wrenching the reins with a little girl holding onto his arm for dear life. The most horrifying characteristic of the ghostly entity was the massive horse whose eyes glowed like fiery coals.

The reverend's nag got spooked by the approaching chaise and threw him from his saddle onto the back of the ghostly bay. The reverend screamed in terror at the demon horse as it bolted up the great rock with a flash of lightning, throwing the man to the ground.

Samuel Nickles woke up sometime later and the sun was out. His Romeo was calmly grazing on the side of the road. He raised himself up wondering if it had all been a dream when he looked up the rock and to his horror saw cloven hoof prints embedded into the rock as if the devil himself had taken the form of the horse that threw him. For years to come people would congregate at the rock while Reverend Nickles preached of how he met the roaming ghost of Peter Rugg and his carriage drawn by the devil's horse.

The rock still sits off of the new Route 1 in North Kingstown. The hoof prints are as fresh in the stone as the day they were burned there by the unholy creature and its ghostly passengers.

Take Interstate Route 95 to Route 1 North. Just after you pass over the bridge of Route 403 there is a sandlot. Pull into the lot and there is a path off to the right. The rock is a few yards into the woods on the path to the left.

# Scallabrini Villa

The lingering laughter and giggles of children always play in the mind of the parents who raised them. Long after the sons and daughters have become adults, the imaginary laughter still fills the minds of the ones who nurtured them. In this case, the sounds of the children are not imaginary, even though the children are long gone.

Scallabrini Villa was once a home to Rhode Island Hospital Children's Facility. It is now rumored haunted by the spirits of the children who died there. The voices of the children playing, laughing, and crying can be heard throughout the older building of the complex. Room 103 is said to host the most ghostly activity. It may have been where the terminally ill children were kept. It could also have been the playroom for the young patients. The current administration has not experienced anything in the way of children's spectral visitations for some time. It would appear that the transformation of the building by its new tenants might have released the sad spirits who were bound to the old hospital as their last home.

You see, the old building, along with a newer one, are now used as retirement homes for nuns and priests under the direction of the Scallabrini Fathers. Could the presence of the pious have given the children eternal peace?

The Villa is located at 860 North Quidnessett Road. Take Interstate Route 95 to Exit 8, Route 2 South. Bear left onto Route 401. Bear right onto Route 1 South, then take a right onto Essex Avenue to North Quidnessett Road.

# Quidnessett Cemetery

The cemetery on School Street off of Post Road (Route 1) is said to be extremely haunted ... and with good reason. For as you drive along the roads of the vast burial ground, you will come to an area of curious report. Sitting in front of some brush is a large stone with a plaque on it. The plaque reads, "ERECTED A.D. 1941 TO MARK THE BURIAL IN THIS PLOT OF THE REMAINS OF FIFTY-FOUR UNIDENTIFIED BODIES MOVED HERE FROM OLD BURIAL PLOTS LOCATED ON LAND ACQUIRED BY THE GOVERNMENT FOR THE SITE OF THE UNITED STATES NAVAL AIR STATION AT QUONSET POINT, R.I."

Quonset Point was built as a strategic air and naval command point overlooking the Narragansett Bay. With the Untied States entering into World War II, coastal defense was top priority. Many homes and farms were commandeered for military use in Rhode Island during this time. The people of the Ocean State were all too glad to see their land under such protection but maybe they were not expecting the discourteous altercations over the government's acts.

It would appear that the government took over the land with little regard to the interred. Replacing each headstone was a task that they were not about to embark on, so they made a common grave for the people they had dug up. That is where they now lay nameless and all but forgotten. It is no wonder they are now seen wandering among the stones of the graveyard, looking for their last piece of immortality ... their headstones.

Residents of the area shy from the cemetery in the hours of darkness, knowing what is lurking within. Many people have witnessed the nightshades of the dead appearing in the area of the common grave. They have also seen strange lights emanating from the spot when there is no visible means to create them.

This is reputed one of the most haunted cemeteries in the state. Maybe someone should have been more diligent in making sure the plots were moved properly and respectfully. Quonset Point is now closed, but the

ERECTED A. D. 1941
TO MARK THE BURIAL
IN THIS PLOT OF THE
REMAINS OF FIFTY-FOUR
UNIDENTIFIED BODIES
MOVED HERE FROM OLD
BURIAL PLOTS LOCATED
ON LAND ACQUIRED
BY THE GOVERNMENT
FOR THE SITE OF THE
UNITED STATES
NAVAL AIR STATION AT
QUONSET POINT, R.I.

Plaque in Quidnesset

grave created in North Kingstown seems to be ceaselessly open.

Quidnessett Cemetery is on the corner of School Street in the northern part of the town off Post Road, also known as Route 1. (See above for detailed directions.)

## Smith's Castle

It is said that a man's home is his castle. This may hold true but not every home is haunted. It seems that every castle is haunted and if that is

the case, then Smith's Castle also falls into the ranks of the paranormal. This beautifully charming home is not only rich with American history, it is plentiful with some of the lingering spirits who forged those memorable moments in time.

It was a crisp autumn day as my wife and I went to visit one of the "Plantation Days" held at the castle. It was on that Sunday afternoon when various members of the historical society and re-enactors in period clothing related the stories and history of the house to us.

The history of the Homestead goes as far back as 1637 when Roger Williams and Richard Smith established a trading post on the land. Roger Williams was the founder of Providence when he and a band of other

Area where eerie lights
have allegedly been seen.

religious and political refugees broke away from the Plymouth Colony in 1636. They settled in what is now Rhode Island. Richard Smith migrated to present day North Kingstown to build a home there. Being on the water, it seemed perfect for trade until the outbreak of King Philip's War in 1675. There had already been Indian attacks upon the land and, fearing for his family, he built tunnels that ran under the house and out to Rabbit Island very close by.

The Indians burned the house down during the war but it was rebuilt in 1678. The eighteenth century saw it become a thriving plantation and slave-holding estate. During the Revolutionary War, soldiers stayed at the secluded territory and, according to historians of the manor, a few skirmishes on the land resulted in the untimely demise of some soldiers during both the Revolutionary War and King Philip's War one hundred years before.

The historic landmark has seen many an unfortunate fate befall it. The ghosts of the castle seem to be trapped in an eternal struggle to right the negative energy that holds them to the homestead. Phantoms of people in colonial attire have been seen wandering through various rooms. Some appear out of nowhere then vanish into thin air. Various witnesses have seen a soldier in a revolutionary uniform walking along the grounds near the water. Perhaps he was one who met a sad fate at the house or he is looking out to sea for something. His ethereal presence is semi-transparent. Noises from inside the house give the curators and other guests a start as many times such noise emanates in the room they are in.

Voices and sound of items falling have been heard by a few of the re-enactors we talked with. If that is not enough to make you sheepish about venturing through the house unaccompanied, there are the re-

Smith's Castle.

ports of phantom slaves who died while hiding in the escape tunnels below the house. The tunnels have long been closed due to their dangerously frail condition, yet the moans of the past and the apparitions of the slaves still permeate the walls and air of the ancient building.

Smith's Castle is a great place to visit, even if you don't see the four centuries of the "other" living history.

The house is located at 55 Richard Smith Drive off Route 1. Follow the same directions as for the places above. The house is closed from mid-December to mid-April. Call (401) 294-3521 for more details.

# Portsmouth
## The Condemning Spirit of
## Rebecca Cornell

The next story you are about to read is a very unusual one. It is the only time in American history where a spirit from beyond the grave provided the evidence that damned her murderer. The accounts of the testimony and trial still exist in the Portsmouth historical records.

Rebecca Cornell was found burned to death in the bedroom of her Portsmouth home on February 8, 1673. It was considered a tragic and untimely accidental death. She loved to smoke her pipe by the fire in the evening after dinner. Each night she would sit in her room rocking to and fro in front of the fireplace with her favorite pipe and tobacco, winding down from the long day's chores.

Authorities assumed that her shawl might have caught fire when she leaned towards the fire to rekindle her smoking vessel. She was mourned and buried, but not too long after her funeral her brother, John Briggs, rode into Newport from his home in Portsmouth to alert the Magistrate of an urgent matter regarding the death of his sister. The magistrate listened in apprehension as John Briggs retold the frightening experience he had. The ghost of his sister, Rebecca, had entered his room the night before. Although the figure was badly burned, he recognized the glowing apparition as his sister from her outline and her voice as she spoke. "Look at me," she said. "See how I am badly burned over my body." She then reached over with her charred hand and pulled her shroud open revealing a hole in her chest that she said was the wound that killed her.

As extraordinary as it may have been, the Magistrate believed the shaken man's story and decided to ride out to Portsmouth and reinvestigate. The local constable and Magistrate dug up Mrs. Cornell's body and to their horror, they found beneath the scars and charred flesh, a gaping hole in her chest. The accidental death was now turned into a murder investigation. Their prime suspect was her son, Thomas Cornell.

Thomas was a sort of "n'er do well" individual who did not work. He lived off of the sole support of his mother. Records also say that he was a heavy drinker with a quick temper. When the authorities went to search the Cornell home, they allegedly found a broken piece of spinning wheel hidden in the house. Thomas was arrested and put on trial for the murder of his mother.

The authorities plausible theory was that Thomas went upstairs to challenge his mother on the fact that she wanted to sell the house and move away. It is possible an argument ensued and Thomas, in a drunken rage, broke the spinning wheel, then used the jagged piece to kill his mother. After seeing what he had done, he dragged the body over to the fireplace and burned it, knowing that everyone was aware that she often smoked her pipe over a crackling blaze. Thomas almost got away with the evil deed until her ghost confided in her beloved brother.

During the trial, the jagged piece of the wheel was presented as well as other witnesses who testified that Mrs. Cornell was in fear for her life because she was planning to move to Pennsylvania and her son was in fear of not getting a share of the proceeds from the sale of the house. The strongest testimony was that of John Briggs, who spoke on behalf of his sister's ghost. Based on witnesses, the jagged piece of wheel, and the spectral testimony of Rebecca's ghost, Thomas Cornell was convicted of murder and sentenced to death.

He was hung in the town square in front of the Old Colony House in Newport. Rebecca now rests quietly in the Cornell burial plot on the Cornell Homestead in Portsmouth. There is a strange epilogue to this story. Guess who are descendants of the Cornell family? Andrew, Emma, and Lizzie Borden. Kind of makes you wonder …

The Portsmouth Town Hall is on Main Street, Route 138 near the junction of West Main Street. For more information, call (401) 683-2101

# Hessian Hole

The largest battle of the Revolutionary War was fought in Portsmouth on August 29, 1778, near Barker's Bloody Brook. The brook gained its name from the fierce battle that left many dead and the brook running red with blood for several days after the struggle. It is presently the site of the Portsmouth Abby.

Some thirty to sixty Hessian soldiers were reported buried in a mass grave by a willow tree. Although the tree is long gone, the large depression in the ground still marks the final resting place of the soldiers. The only problem is they are not at rest. On a foggy night one can unmistakably see the phantoms of the tall Hessian soldiers solemnly marching towards the western sky.

The exact location of the sunken grave is lost to time. Some reports say that it is located on the Abby grounds near Barker's Brook where the Carnegie Golf Course now stands. Another report by the *Providence Journal*

*Almanac* over one hundred years ago puts it in the Lehigh State Picnic Grove just off Route 114. A Works Progress and Administration *Guide To Rhode Island and Massachusetts,* published in 1937, states it is closer to Route 114.

If you are in the area of these locations, look for the large depression in the ground and wait for the moon to rise over the land. There you will see the soldiers once again marching into eternity.

Take Interstate Route 95 to Exit 8, Route 2 South. Route 2 will merge with Route 4 South. Take Route 138 East over the Jamestown Bridge and then over the Newport Bridge. There is a toll for the Newport Bridge. Follow Route 138 to Route 114 North. It will be in the area of Route 114 and Brown's Lane. .

# Providence

## The Wandering Ghosts of
## Benefit Street

Providence's Benefit Street stirs up reminiscences of centuries past. The brick sidewalks and gas streetlights still grace this outstanding section of the Capitol City. It's no wonder the people and entities of the past centuries still linger on long after their time has gone.

This historic street was once home to many prominent names in our country. Certain paranormal investigators believe this street to be the most haunted place in Rhode Island.

Among the numerous ghosts is an eighteenth century horse drawn carriage that has been seen by several people pulling up to a house, then

A shot of historical Benefit Street of Providence's extravagant East Side, where numerous ghosts are said to roam.

vanishing. The phantom coach makes no sound as it glides along the street. Even the horse's hooves are silent as they are seen traveling down the ancient thoroughfare. A man dressed in black has been witnessed walking up and down the street. Also, the tapping of a woman's heels on the sidewalk might mean the spirit of a woman in nineteenth century garb is close by. No one knows who these people were in life. They only know that they are making their mark in a time long after they were gone.

There have been sightings of an old woman spying out of an attic window in one of the old houses and even Edgar Allen Poe, who spent a portion of his life on Benefit Street when he was engaged to Sarah Helen Whitman, has been witnessed walking the sidewalks in the early hours of dawn. Many witnesses have heard footsteps approach the Whitman house, then stop. Others have actually seen the semi-transparent form with the stature of a man walking in the vicinity of the house. The figure usually vanishes when they get close but some have actually gotten close enough to verify that it did in fact resemble Edgar Allen Poe before fading into the night air. The area of Benefit Street is home to Brown University and Rhode Island School of Design so there are many credible witnesses from students to professors who have seen, heard, or felt the presence of the ghosts of Benefit Street.

To walk the brick sidewalks of the street and gaze at the historic homes is a treat in itself. If you happen to look beside you and have an unexpected guest in nineteenth century attire walking silently along with you, well, that's an added bonus.

Benefit Street is on Providence's lavish East Side. Take Interstate Route 95 to Route 195 East. Take the Gano Street exit and then the first left onto Wickenden Street. Follow Wickenden Street to Benefit Street and bear left onto Benefit Street.

# Rhode Island School of Design

Some schools have more school spirit than others. This one seems to have more spirits than any other institution of higher learning. Several of the buildings on campus are reputed haunted for one reason or another. Many have no explanation as students stay such a short time in these quarters. They never get to settle enough to learn what might really cause them to have to live with unseen and sometimes seen entities from the other side.

Farnum Hall is reported haunted by several ghosts. They range from friendly to malevolent. Students have been awoken in the middle of the night by an apparition standing over their bed looking at them. The figure will vanish suddenly when they go to grab it. Heavy footsteps in the halls have brought many an alumni to their doors only to see the walkway empty of the living. Voices in the rooms from invisible mouths have spooked even the bravest from the building. The nature of the haunting is not known.

They tell me the Nightingale House has a very busy ghost. The lounge is the target of this unseen prankster. It moves furniture around and even turns the lights off on the students while sitting in the room. A student took a picture of the building and was astonished to find orbs in the photograph in front of the house.

The Dunnel House holds a vengeful spirit within its walls. It takes its anger out by knocking things over and causing intense cold spots in the rooms. The spirit has also been seen by almost everybody in the house. They described it as a shadow-like figure that glides eerily along the walls. Even more frightening than that is the face of a woman who has appeared in the window of the second floor stairwell. Could they be one in the same? No one has had the courage to ask.

In the Dexter House the residents say many spirits roam the halls and basement. They are not frightening, just seemingly lost. This would seem more apt as the building was once a morgue. Maybe the entities do not know they are dead.

If you enter the Barstow House, be sure to concentrate on the red and turquoise rooms. Within each room people experience sudden cold spots and abrupt feelings of depression with a need to make a hasty exit. The hue in both rooms is always gloomy. There are also large mirrors that have reflected the image of someone passing by when looking into them. When the person turns around, there is no one in sight.

Homer Hall is a multi-sectioned living quarter with its share of ghosts. One section has two ghosts. One is a male who is frequently seen in the bathroom. He also plays with stereos and breaks things. It is rumored that a student committed suicide some thirty years ago by jumping from the top balcony of the recently constructed building. No one was cooperative enough or was there at that time to confirm that story and there exists no other documentation to substantiate the rumor. You can make your own conclusion on this one. The other is the ghost of a woman who likes to turn on the faucets in the girl's bathroom. Students claim to have been startled by strange shadows moving about the lounge in the house.

Of all the buildings that are reputed haunted at RISD, it seems the Pardon Miller off-campus house is the most popular. Students share the house with what seems to be a family of three that has stayed behind long after they were given back to the earth. Two small children have been witnessed in the basement playing, unconscious of their wide-eyed observers. They appear and disappear at random. Upstairs, occupants frequently hear the voice of a woman talking. There is no explanation for the phantom voice and it is barely understandable as it echoes through the hallways and rooms.

Why are so many buildings at Rhode Island School of Design haunted? Like many other urban colleges and universities, they buy up old houses in the middle of the city and renovate them to suit their needs. Whether or not they come with a history that would cause them to be haunted takes a back seat or is even lost in their original mission. It is not the concern of the school. It seems in this case, with all the ghosts that reside in these buildings for free, they could make a few extra bucks on the boos.

Rhode Island School of Design is located on Providence's East Side. Follow directions for Benefit Street and you will see the buildings scattered along the streets.

# Swan Point Cemetery

Ghosts and cemeteries go hand in hand. It seems that every cemetery has at least one ghost story entombed within its walls. The bigger the graveyard, the more chance of ghouls drifting among the stones under a full moon. Swan Point Cemetery is not only a spectral treat but a historic one as well. You can probably guess that some of the prominent figures buried here are among the apparitions seen in the burial ground as well.

Swan Point was founded in 1846. At that time there was a trend towards landscaped open cemeteries where people could visit loved ones in a more pleasing atmosphere. Garden cemeteries offered rural dwellers a place to escape as well. To this day many people jog, hike, walk their pets, and even picnic in these landscaped rolling hills of green. It almost assures the owners of the necropolis a kind of potential clientele for the future. What most might love in life, they would want for eternity.

Rhode Island was primarily farmland and every farm had a family burial plot. As a matter of fact, Rhode Island has more burial grounds than any other state in the United States, an amazing fact when you consider its diminutive size. Swan Point presently covers two hundred acres and offers scenery to die for. Some of the dead like it enough to wander the grounds with the living.

Buried here are such notables as Thomas Dorr, the rebel Governor of Rhode Island, who helped change the peoples voting rights in the state. He died in prison after a rebellion about the Governorship was quelled. There is good reason why he would not rest. He never took office, despite being voted in by a newly formed People's Party. The Sprague family was the richest family in the state, with members who were governors and senators. (See Sprague Mansion.) William Sprague met an untimely death when he choked on a fish bone and Amasa was murdered near his home on December 31, 1843. His ghost has been seen near the great mausoleum bearing the family name.

Ambrose Everett Burnside was a general in the Civil War. His famous tufts of facial hair along the sides of his head gave birth to the phrase, "sideburns." He was not a very good strategist and that is why he probably haunts the grounds, looking for redemption and respect for his mili-

Entrance to Swan Point Cemetery.

tary blunders. Many witnesses claim to have seen a spectral figure near a gravestone with a cannonball mounted on top of it. That might be the spirit of John Rogers Vinton, who was killed in the Mexican War by the very cannonball that sits upon his marker.

All the spirits of Swan Point are not historically famous. There are some that are seen in the old section where no one ventures after dark unless they are ready to be terrified out of their wits. In general there have been many sightings of numerous paranormal incidents in every area of the cemetery, but the most interesting is in the area of the Phillip's

Sprague family mausoleum at Swan Point.

monument. It is here, along with his family, that the great writer of horror, Howard Phillips Lovecraft, is buried.

H.P. Lovecraft left an immortal legacy of stories that even to this day chill the very marrow of those who read them. His untimely death on March 15, 1937, at the age of only forty-seven might explain why he would be seen roaming among his family plot. Scores of people claim to have seen Lovecraft's ghost near his grave.

Carl Johnson, who is a leading authority on the history and life of H.P. Lovecraft, does a memorial service and seminar for the writer at his gravesite every year around the time of his death. He claims he has never seen the writer's ghost but would be very pleased if the master of the macabre showed up while

Gravestone of H.P. Lovecraft in the Phillip's family plot.

he was there. For information on attending the gathering, you can e-mail him at Constablecj@hotmail.com. It is free and very interesting to attend.

What makes the ghosts of Swan Point meander so freely among the graves when the spirits of the living are always rambling about carelessly, taking in the atmosphere around their eternal domain? Maybe they have taken refuge in the famous words of Carl Johnson, "Mock not the crows of Swan Point for they are the guardians of those souls which here linger..."

Swan Point is located at Blackstone Boulevard. Follow directions for Benefit Street. Take right onto Angell Street to Blackstone Boulevard.

Entrance to the cemetery is easy to spot. Guards are posted after hours, so please respect the closing time. For more information, call (401) 272-1314.

# Brown University

University Hall at Brown University is the oldest building on the campus. It was built in 1770 and houses a number of ghosts from the past before it was even a college.

University Hall occupies the very same parcel of land that once held a horse stable. A secretary by the name of Melissa Bartini once related in an interview how she heard the distinct sound of a horse walking around in the basement. Not knowing what to make of it, she checked the strange sounds out. She was even more amazed when she found the basement was completely empty, save for the old files that had been stored there. Students and visitors have seen an old man leading a horse towards the building, only to disappear through the wall.

As Susan Smitten relates in her book, *Ghost Stories of New England*, a former alumni, Mary Karlsson, tells of a ghost in the building who loves to move furniture. The spirit has been blamed for moving an enormous bookcase to the center of a room that was allegedly locked up. She knows of another spirit, this one a man, who steals records and files. They have also heard him crying in empty offices. One day an employee was upstairs cleaning. She went to dust a frame and spied the reflection of a man in period clothing behind her. When she whirled around there was no one in the hall.

There is a story of how some students at the library across the street once saw a ghost in one of the offices on the second floor. Workers have reported the same sighting. The apparition has occurred often enough that they have named the ghost, "Elizabeth."

People actually come to the building and sit vigil, waiting for something supernatural to take place right in front of them. There is a ghostly tour of Providence hosted by local historian Rory Raven. There is a special Halloween tour as well. The tour includes the great hall that has made so many students and faculty believers in other subjects than what is in their curriculum.

University Hall at Brown University where a number of ghosts, including a horse, are said to reside.

Not all of the employees of the building believe there is paranormal activity lurking about. Although they find some things hard to explain, they still have found rational explanations for many things. It's the events you just read about that make them wonder who else will be at work with them on any given day.

Brown University is located on the East Side of Providence along such streets as Thayer, Brook, Benefit, and Waterman. For more information, call (401) 863-1600.

# Scituate

## Black Horse Tavern

There once stood in the middle of Scituate Village a tavern called the Black Horse. A man named Reuben Jenckes owned the expansive hostelry.

As the story goes, the ghost of a Narragansett Indian haunted the building because he preferred the nearby Pine Tree Tavern in life and wanted the business to migrate there. Another version says he haunted the Jenckes family out of embarrassment.

The ghost haunted the family in the form of violent dreams. He would be seen by various members of the family pointing to someplace in the dream followed by some sort of horrific nightmare.

The ghost once led Reuben's daughter, Lucy Jenckes, to a loft in the carriage house where a coffin containing a dressmaking doll was found. It is rumored that in a drunken stupor, the Indian tried to scalp the doll, thinking it was a rude person who would not return his conversation. The ghost requested that she remove the doll from the scene of the crime. She removed the doll and the haunting supposedly ceased. Guests of the tavern still insisted the Indian stayed behind, as many were jolted out of a sound sleep in the night by frightening war cries. Some have even been pulled out of bed by the hair.

The tavern was used as a meeting house and local party place. The second floor held ample amounts of revelers making merry until all hours of the night. There were other owners of the tavern so the exact timeline of the haunting is unclear in records.

Deeds to such small towns with farming origins can become quite vague. What is clear is that licenses, which read for "Tavern, Ale, and Victualing House," were handed out to early settlers like the Potters, Manchesters, Smiths, and Hopkins in the mid-eighteenth century. Reuben Jenckes probably owned the Black Horse after 1800.

Since the structure is no longer a tavern, it seems the spirit has gotten its way and the haunting has allegedly subsided. The building is now a deli serving very tempting delights. Maybe tempting enough for the ghost to come back.

The deli is at the intersection of Danielson Pike and Route 116 (East Road). Take Interstate Route 295 to Exit 6, Route 6, Hartford. Follow

Supposed site of the former Black Horse Tavern.

into Scituate where the road becomes Danielson Pike, Route 6, to intersection of Route 116.

## Unknown Pasture

There is a pasture along the Scituate Reservoir that is shunned by animals. A washerwoman appears and disappears there as well. I believe the pasture might be near 116 and Central Avenue just outside of Scituate Center.

The location of the pasture is vague as the reservoir covers a vast amount of land. To get to the reservoir, follow above directions and take a left onto Route 116. This will take you around the reservoir loop.

# The Hanging Tree

This particular tree is not only the oldest tree in Rhode Island, but it also has sealed many a villain's fate. The massive branches that once draped outward over the field are now gone. Its mammoth trunk still reaches up to the sky but is also beginning to fall away with time. The tree has many stories imprinted within it. There are also the vengeful ghosts that the tree claimed when it was a hangman's tree many years ago.

The hanging tree in Scituate. Although the tree is long dead, the ghosts of the tree still echo in the wind. Many of the massive limbs have fallen from the tree.

The tree is almost four hundred years old. The early settlers of the area saw the potential of the then large oak for use as a hanging tree. The remnants of the two colossal hanging branches are strewn across the ground around the tree. The tree is fenced in but is still a public viewing place. It is said that voices of the past break through the time barrier and can be heard on occasion. If you are there on a moonlit night you might also see shadows dangling from what is left of the massive branches.

The tree is located on Route 14 just before Crazy Corners. Follow directions above to Route 116 and take a right onto Route 14 from Route 116.

# Smithfield
## Resolved Waterman Tavern

Spirits are said to haunt places where a tragic event took place. By all records that theory seems to hold true. Sometimes a spirit can be released when the reason behind the haunting is unearthed. In this case, however, the person behind the haunting was never found.

The Greenville Tavern, as it came to be called, was built in 1733 by a man named Resolved Waterman on the Putnam Pike. The Waterman family became one of the prominent names responsible for settling the northwestern part of Rhode Island. The inn was "T" shaped with an eastern ell and a western ell connected by a cobble courtyard. Because it was located on the only main stage run through that part of the state, it was a hot spot for locals and travelers alike. The tavern contained a large banquet hall on

The haunted Resolve Waterman Tavern in Greenville. Once slated for demolition, the ghost and building have been saved for future renovation.

the first floor of the western ell with a dance hall on the second floor directly above it.

The place was so popular that it rarely stayed vacant. One evening a weary traveling peddler came to the inn in need of a room but there were none to be had. Mr. Waterman felt bad for the man and gave him quarters in the only place that was empty, the root cellar.

The contented peddler ate and sat at the bar for some spirits before retiring for the night. When the time came to close the tavern, he stumbled to his room to sleep off the grog he had consumed. He was never seen again. The next morning the tavern keeper found his bag of wares near where he had bedded for the night but the peddler was gone.

The only explanation they could come up with was that the man, in his drunken condition, began wandering around in the dark cellar and fell into the deep well. They checked the well as best they could but did not come up with any evidence to support their theory. Resolved allegedly closed up the well and dug a new one in a safer spot. Shortly after, people began seeing the ghost of the peddler in the tavern.

His specter was witnessed wandering about the rooms by many startled guests and patrons who recognized the nightshade as that of the unknown peddler they had shared drinks with on that fateful night. A regular of the pub once saw a white figure cross the pantry and float into the kitchen. It frightened him so much he made an illustration of the apparition. The drawing hung over the bar for many years afterward. Another boarder staying in a room in the cellar once saw a pair of scissors rise up and fly towards him. Needles to say, the terrified guest hastily grabbed his belongings and fled for his life.

Time passed and the inn changed hands. Notable names like Whipple, Evans, McLaughlin, and Mowry would own the haunted building at some point. In 1936, the front section of the building was torn down to make room for the expansion of Putnam Pike. The last inhabitant of the house was Mrs. Bessie Fish. It was reported that the ghostly activity was going on right up to the time the house was willed to Cumberland Farms™ store chain in the early 1970s. The ghost was alone in the house until 2003.

In 2003, the Smithfield Historical Society obtained the decrepit building with the intentions of restoring it and making it into a museum. Once again it will become a public place for people to browse around and take in some small town history. You might even get a tour from a ghostly figure resembling an eighteenth century peddler.

The tavern is located on Route 44 in Greenville, a small hamlet of Smithfield. Take Interstate Route 295 to Exit 7, Greenville. Follow Route 44 West for about two miles and the building will be on your right just before the fire station.

# The Lost City

Ghost towns are rare in the present day. If you find one you can bet that it is probably haunted. Such is the case of Hanton City, an abandoned town in the middle of the woods in the north part of Smithfield. The three thousand acre parcel is also known as Island Woods. The old roads that lace through the deserted village are still on the state map as thoroughfares. They are thought to be the oldest in the state. The roads are rough and unpaved but the voices and people of the past still echo through the overgrowth that has taken their homes in the passage of time. Old timers in the area still tell of the demise and spirits that haunt Hanton City.

Hanton City was a thriving community that became extinct around 1836. All that remain are wells, cellar holes, stone walls, cemeteries, and a threshing rock used to winnow grain along Aldrich Trail and Hanton City Trail. Travelers used to pass through the town on their way to present day Woonsocket. The trip was a long one. Long enough where the people of Hanton City built a small shack and put some rum and bread in it for the weary trekker to rest and quench his hunger. It is said that everyone who took advantage of the settlement's hospitality always left a monetary token of appreciation.

According to the records, the old fashioned pronunciation for Harrington was Hanton. The townsfolk were shoemakers and tanners. They also quarried the stone that lay abundantly about the settlement. Remains of the village can be seen along the two trails.

As better ways to get from town to town were devised, Hanton City became a wayside village. The new Route 7 was built as a shortcut to Woonsocket and the town was all but forgotten. The residents became bitter and poor. Local residents attest to the fact that the whole settlement was wiped out by disease. There are no real records kept on the village and no descendants who had relatives living there. Through what little history I could find on the lost city, this seems like the most plausible explanation for how the village met its ruin. It could also attribute to why it is haunted. The crumbling stone buildings were then used as hideouts for the Underground Railroad. There is even a wall with a small room built in it where slaves could hide on their way to freedom. After the Civil War only the buried remained in Hanton City. All these ruins are among the only untouched artifacts in all New England.

Strange occurrences have been reported by many who have gone up to the foreboding village. Indian spirits have repelled hunters from their burial mounds. It has been told that the spirits of the Indians buried up there protect their grave mounds. Anyone who veers too close to the tombs is physically repelled by an unseen force. Especially discouraged are hunters with rifles. (There is an occasional hunter scouring the woods during deer season). I guess the natives still hold a grudge against the White Man and his "fire-stick."

Voices of the past have been heard in the woods when no one else is around. The moans of a child have been heard even in broad daylight. The voices seem to emanate from everywhere in the woods as if the town is still alive with the workings of the nineteenth century. Day or night is a good time to witness the ghostly phenomena. Daytime is recommended though.

At night the howling of coyotes serves as a warning to all who would dare enter the lost city after the sun has set. There is a foundation where hikers have claimed to see a ghost floating around. It is on the left as you enter the village. The local residents have dubbed it the "Hermit's House."

My wife and I lived for a short time on the edge of Hanton City. The trail ran along side the property into the woods where a swamp had claimed a section of it. The trail then picks up past the bog into the thicket. At night sounds of the most eerie sort could be heard emerging from the woods near the city. We only ventured towards the village a few times in the dark and never went too far into the ethereal woods. I never saw anything ghostly in the wooded area, but I must say I was spooked several times by what sounded like people talking around me. The old farm we lived on is gone, as the land was sold for industrial purposes, but the city and access road still remain as well as some of its inhabitants many years after they have passed on. Take a walk down Hanton City Trail and see for yourself that the abandoned town is peopled still.

Take Interstate Route 295 to Exit 8, North Smithfield. Go straight through the

The Greenville Public Library as it looks today.

132

intersection of Routes 7 and 116. Take the first right onto Lydia Ann Drive. Most of the trails have to be traversed by foot. The adjoining property along the road is private so stay in the lane.

# Greenville Public Library's
# Permanent Librarian

When the Jenckes family gave this piece of land to the town for a library they had a barn, house, and other outbuildings. The town tore

down several of those buildings for the new library but left the family home intact. When you pull into the library parking lot you will see the house behind the bushes that run along the back of the building. The family lived in the house long after the library was built. They carefully watched over the library's affairs to ensure it was run according to the citizens of Greenville's wishes. If that is the case then, they remain watchful now, but in another form.

When the library was built, a beautiful stone building was also donated for storage and conferences. The town eventually tore the building down and expanded the parking lot. This may have set off old Mrs. Jenckes, who was a longtime trustee of the library and donator of the land in 1938. The present building was commissioned on October 18, 1955.

The basement of this building seems to be the most haunted. Many patrons have reported the uncanny feeling of being watched by some unseen presence while in the lower floor of the library. There is a piano in one of the lower chambers that has been heard playing when no one was in that particular room. These occurrences take place at random hours throughout the day and night. Darryll Aucoin is one of the former members of the staff at the library who credits Mrs. Jenckes for the ghostly deeds. Some nights he would turn all the lights off downstairs and by the time he was back on the first floor, they were all on again. Books would fall from the shelves in front of the staff as if an unseen hand was pulling them from their resting place.

Once he and a girl witnessed a whole row of books slide out of the shelf onto the floor like someone had taken an arm and pushed them from behind. Some say it might be the spirit of a former librarian. Orra Angell was the first librarian for the village in 1882 when the library was down the street across from the common. Maybe she has migrated with her books to the newer location, still making sure they are kept in good order. Whoever it may be, much of the staff would never venture down into the lower catacombs unaccompanied for fear of what they might encounter while alone down there.

The library is located at 573 Putnam Pike just before Greenville Common across from William Winsor Elementary School. Follow the previous directions to Route 44. Building is about one mile from Interstate Route 295.

# South Kingstown
## Rose Hill Cemetery

What exactly constitutes a vampire? The body of the undead who rises from the tomb in the realm of darkness to feed upon the lifeblood of a living creature. In the end that poor creature is soon to become the same eternal wanderer of the damned. This is an eerie but accurate definition based on what we have seen in movies or read in books. In nineteenth century Rhode Island it seems vampires were of a different definition. They were in the form of young children who had succumbed to consumption. Now they would leave the grave on the darkest of nights and slowly bring their families to their side from the living.

At least that is what William Rose of Peacedale might have thought. When members of his family began to mysteriously waste away beyond medical rationale he sought to find the culprit. It was in 1874 that he had his fifteen year old daughter exhumed for fear that she was a vampire. She had been the first to die of the strange disease and it seemed to him that she was the ghoul causing the others to be called to their graves at the midnight tolling. Her heart was cut out and burned in the usual New England fashion for exorcising a vampire. Where she was re-interred is unknown. The family is buried in the Rose Hill Cemetery near the gates. Yet there is no marker bearing any evidence that their daughter is buried among them.

Where is she and what did they really do with her?

Rose Hill Cemetery is on Rose Hill Road off of Route 138 (Moorefield Road). Take Interstate Route 95 to Route 102 South. Take Route 1 South to Mooresfield Road across from the Hannah Robinson Tower. Take a right and follow to Rose Hill Road.

## Crying Bog

Legend has it that a Narragansett Indian squaw named Manouna strangled her two children. Reasons why she killed them are unknown but she buried them in the marsh to cover up her crime. Her spirit now roams the marsh mourning her misdeed. Many witnesses have claimed to hear her cries coming from the bog. There are even reports of her ghost being seen near the side of the road moaning over the loss of her children.

Crying Bog is located at the corners of Route 1 and Route 108. Take Interstate Route 95 South to Route 102 South. Take Route 1 South into Wakefield.

# University Of Rhode Island's
# Smart Ghosts

Some of the ghosts that haunt the walls of this great university were not even old enough to be in school. Maybe they were there long before the school was. Either way, here are some of the scary and smart ghosts of URI.

The Chi Omega Sorority House is haunted by the spirit of a woman who plays with doors and windows on the third floor. She has been witnessed on the fire escape as well. People have heard voices in the house when it was supposedly empty. The ghost is of unknown origin. The Will Theatre, Theatre J, had an incident where an unseen set of hands recently pushed a teacher down the stairs. No one else was in the theatre at the time. The Theta Delta Chi Fraternity is reported haunted by a spirit named Barbara and a little child. The child has been seen bouncing a ball on the third floor of the house.

The land the school is on was once the Oliver Watson Farm until the state bought it and built a school there in 1888. The original farmhouse, fully restored, still stands on the university grounds. The Alpha Phi Sorority House is the house that is haunted by a ghost named Patrick. He was the son of the man who built the house. He lets the tenants know he is there by throwing shelves, playing with the water faucets, and banging doors. All these are enough to make a student's study a bit unnerving, but the most haunted building on campus seems to be the Sigma Phi House.

The Sigma Phi Fraternity House has the reputed haunting of a mysterious nature. A long time friend and former university alumni, Kevin Fay, related the following accounts to me. One of his frat brothers was removing his contact lenses. He had just gotten the first one stowed away when a face appeared in front of him. The bodiless apparition hovered within hands reach of the frightened young scholar. He let out a yell and the face disappeared. After a few more sightings of the ghostly face, he moved to another room. Another brother claimed to have seen the eerie face several times as well. It would suddenly appear out of nowhere, stare into the air for a few moments, and then vanish. He too had the same room. One of his frat mates was studying one night while his girlfriend slept on his bed. A strange feeling made him suddenly turn around. To his alarm he saw a dark figure leaning over the girl as if trying to hug her. He sprang towards the form as it stood upright and then faded away. Even a former cook heard noises coming from that room when he was absolutely sure no one was there. No one knows who the spirit may be. There are no records of tragic circumstances surrounding the house on campus. There is one interesting epilogue.

The Sigma Phi National Headquarters in Vincennes, Indiana, is haunted as well as the Sigma Phi House in Gettysburg, Pennsylvania. It might be a fraternity rite of passage from this world to the next.

The University of Rhode Island is located on Route 138 West. Follow directions to Rose Hill Road but stay on Route 138. The University is a few miles further.

# Hannah Robinson Rock

The life of Hannah Robinson was one of love, betrayal, and tragedy. Her story is part of Rhode Island's rich history, as is her haunting as well. Hannah Robinson was born in 1746. Her father, Howland Robinson, was a very wealthy plantation owner. She spent many of her childhood days sitting on a rock gazing out at the scenic vistas of the Narragansett Bay. There she found great peace in the countless hours she spent on that cube-shaped rock near her Boston Neck (Narragansett) home.

In 1765, the nineteen-year-old Hannah was sent to a ladies school in Newport for formal education at the will of her father. It was there that she met and fell in love with Peter Simon, who was a teacher at the academy. They started a secret courtship, knowing that Hannah's father would never approve of her dating a common teacher. The affair continued even after her schooling was completed with the help of some close relatives and friends. It wasn't long before Hannah's father caught wind of the romance and put an end to it.

Hannah was now a prisoner in her home. Even if she was to venture out of his sight, he made sure she was accompanied by one of his trusted servants. Enough was enough for the stubborn Hannah, who had inherited that trait from her father. She decided to elope. Her mother was quite unhappy with the idea but helped set up the arrangement for her to run away with her love. Hannah's aunt, Mrs. Ludovick Updike, was holding a ball at the Smith's Castle and the timing could not have been better. With the help of her uncle and some friends, the couple stole off into the night to Providence to wed. When her father found out, he was enraged by the fact that his daughter could marry beneath her class. He offered a large reward for the names of the conspirators who helped her get away. No on ever confessed to the deed.

As time passed Peter began to realize that Hannah's father was never going to give them anything in the way of inheritance. At first he was drawn to an attitude of inattention for his wife, then he deserted her altogether. As she became depressed, poverty and illness set in on poor Hannah. She stayed in Providence for a while, still resisting the will of her father to come clean on who helped her on that fateful night. This obstinate feud continued until Hannah was near death. It was at that point that those

who helped her elope came forward and begged her father to forgive her. The father did and dispatched four servants to bring the dying girl home. On the way she asked to stop at the rock she so loved as a child. Once at the stone she pulled up some flowers and sat for quite some time. She was heartbroken and near her end but still found peace in the place where she was always happy. She died shortly thereafter, on October 30, 1773. Hannah was only twenty- seven years old.

Her spirit now roams the rock and grounds that bear her name in memory of her sad and tragic passing. It is in that peaceful place where you will see the ghost of young Hannah Robinson and hear the mournful

sighs echoing in the wind as she relives the last moments of her life forever and ever.

Hannah Robinson Rock is located in the Hannah Robinson Park on Route 1. Take Interstate Route 95 to Route 4 South. Route 4 becomes Route 1. Follow to the junction of Route 138 West. Take a left into the parking lot where the tower is located. Follow a short path through the woods to the ledge where you will find the rock.

Hannah Robinson Rock, where many have reported seeing her mournful spirit roaming the boulder.

# Tiverton
## Sakonnet River

Imagine looking out on the beautiful Sakonnet River just as the sun sets into the water and seeing the shadows of canoes with natives rowing them. That is exactly what some residents along the river have witnessed on many occasions, only the canoes and the Indians are not real.

The phantom canoes carrying the ghostly specters are seen floating down the waterway on occasion. Those who witness the phenomenon have observed that the oars make no wake in the water or sound. They always vanish when confronted.

This seems strange in the modern world but two hundred years ago it was quite normal in those parts to see such a sight on the river. As a matter of a fact, archeological digs along the banks of the Sakonnet have turned up artifacts from many ancient tribes that used to regularly camp along the river. For some strange reason, the phantom tribesmen still roam the grounds where food and fish were plentiful. Could they still be hungry after all this time?

The Sakonnet River separates Tiverton from Portsmouth. Take Interstate Route 95 to Interstate Route 195 East. Take Route 114 South over the Mount Hope Bridge. Bear left onto Route 24 into Tiverton. Take Route 77 along the shore to Nannaquaket Road. The sightings are in this area and happen mostly during the evening.

## Sin and Flesh Brook

Traveling the trails of early New England was a dangerous undertaking. Wolves, bobcats, rattlesnakes, and bear were just some of the potential perils that early settlers faced when journeying from one town to another. Traveling the roads during King Philip's War was downright suicidal. King Philip's War was a brutal and bloody struggle between the colonists during the reign of King Philip in England and various collective tribes under the spearhead of Narragansett sachem, Metacomet.

Such a thought never entered the mind of Zoeth Howland on March 28, 1676, when he mounted his steed and left his Dartmouth, Massachusetts, home to travel to Newport, Rhode Island, for a Quaker meeting. The ever-pious Howland had covered fifteen miles of the thirty-mile trip when he became a casualty of the war. As he rode down the horse path in Tiverton six hostile Indians ambushed him. They murdered the religious man, then threw his mutilated corpse into the brook nearby.

When a group of settlers discovered the mangled body they were mortified. They named the brook "Sinning Flesh River" in remembrance of the horrible deed. Over the years it has been renamed Sin and Flesh Brook but Zoeth still makes his way among the leaves and brush along the banks of the watercourse. People have heard screams from the river and have claimed to even see the river run red with blood. Zoeth has made an appearance to more than one hiker on the trail that still traverses the area where he was killed. If you decide to follow the stream to an area that looks ominous and sinister, look around for the ghosts of six Indians and a lonely rider. You might just see a ghastly piece of history repeat itself.

Sin and Flesh Brook is located on the eastern side of Tiverton. Follow the previous directions. Just past Nannaquaket Road will be Bridgeport Road. Take left onto Bridgeport Road and then right onto Old Main Road. The brook crosses under the road at its starting point, where the little pond on the right is. The trail leads to Fort Barton, the small ruins of a Revolutionary War fort, as it snakes back and forth over the river.

# Warren

## Kickemuit River

Along the misty banks of the Kickemuit River cat o' nine tails emerge from the shores, rising up to the sky. These are permanent fixtures to the

river's shoreline. There is another permanent but not so pleasant example of scenery often seen by people gazing at the eerie waterway. They see the terrifying image of eight severed heads floating along the tree line near the river.

The origin of this haunting goes back to June 20, 1675. Tension had grown between the colonists and the local Indians in the area. This ill feeling between the colonists and natives exploded on June 20, 1675, when a band of Pokanolet warriors attacked the settlement along the banks of the Kickemuit River. They looted and vandalized several homes. Two homes were burned in the attack. On June 23rd the Pokanolet returned to

ransack and burn more houses. John Salisbury shot and wounded one of the Indians as they retreated. The following day they returned to exact revenge for the shooting. The renegade band killed John Salisbury and six other colonists near Swazey Corner during the bloody struggle. Two other men were ambushed and killed as they ran to the nearby settlements for help.

A week after the incident, the severed heads of the murdered colonists were seen on the banks of the river mounted on long poles with gruesome smiles pulled across their faces. This was a clear message to the colonists, "Go home or meet the same fate." The attack on the settlement sparked the brutal and bloody conflict known as King Philip's War between the local Indian tribes and the colonists. There was more violence to come but the innocent colonists who died that day have never left the spot they were hung as a warning.

Several times a year residents of Warren witness eight floating heads above the shore of the river. Most often they are seen about the trees glowing in the twilight hours of early evening. Sometimes they are wit-

Area of the Kickemuit River where the ghoulish apparitions of eight severed heads are seen floating through the air along the shoreline.

nessed on poles in the ground on the edge of the Kickemuit near the bridge that crosses the river at Route 136. Either way, it is a ghastly sight to behold. Witnesses who have seen them say the faces seem to look distressed or forlorn. When you visit the Kickemuit River, take a stroll along the banks. If you get the feeling you are being watched, look to the trees and you might see eight glowing faces staring down at you wondering if you are friend or foe.

The Kickemuit River runs through the center of Warren. Take Interstate Route 195 East to Route 114 East. Bear left where Routes 114 and 103 split. Take Route 136 South off of Route 103.

# Nathaniel Porter Inn

Water Street in Colonial Warren must have been quite a place to live. The quaint cobblestone roads along the water's edge lined with shops and day-trippers who bow their heads to one another as they pass. You can almost see the young children playing in the streets on a warm summer day as keepers sweep their walkways. No wonder some have stayed on to bask in the atmosphere of such a delightful little hamlet. The Nathaniel Porter Inn seems to hold a few of these lingering spirits of another time.

The inn was originally a cooper's shop in 1750. A cooper was a person that made barrels and pails out of wood. They would bend the slats then shape the rings that would hold them together. I once saw a demonstration of how they performed their talents and must admit it was quite a skilled trade in those days. In 1795 Samuel Martin, a ship captain, expanded the structure for living purposes. He named the house in honor of Nathaniel Porter, a twelve-year-old boy who became a local hero when he joined the minutemen at Lexington and Concord in 1775. The Martin family lived in the home until the early twentieth century, when it became a tenement house. It was purchased and rebuilt as an inn around 1980. The establishment serves some of the finest delights this side of the Mississippi. The décor is purely colonial and it is thought that most of the ghosts are as well.

All of the staff has heard voices, both male and female, calling to them or crying when there is no one else around. Guests of the inn have witnessed the glow of a candle moving across the wall in some of the guest rooms. It is thought to be the nightshade of a housekeeper named Martha that was in charge of the rooms from around 1810 to 1823. Lights turn on and off even when the switch is in plain view and not moving. Apparitions have been seen in the dining room on several occasions. A guest once became quite frightened by a wispy figure of a man walking through the dining room. There have been reports of a spirit seen sitting in a chair by one of the guest room windows. She is said to be looking down at the street where her child used to play. The child supposedly met an untimely death. The woman also reportedly fell to her death on the stairs of the inn. She is said to be waiting for her young one to return home. Ghosts of the inn are not shy about visitors. Check out the food and spirits for yourself.

The Nathaniel Porter Inn is located at 125 Water Street in Warren. Take Interstate Route 195 to Route 114 South. It will intersect with Route 103. Follow into Warren and Water Street is on your right.

# Warwick

## Aldrich Mansion

Nelson W. Aldrich built this great estate while a United States senator. Work on the mansion began in 1896 and was finally completed in 1912. He was born poor but worked his way up to an exalted position in U.S. history. The seventy-five acre estate contains the manor, carriage house, caretaker's quarters, and boathouse, all on the edge of the Narragansett Bay. There was also a teahouse that burned down many years ago. It was here that one of his daughters, Abby Aldrich, wed John D. Rockefeller, father of the great Nelson Rockefeller.

The seventy room mansion was surely a sight to behold. The boathouse was no less impressive. It even has a room that resembles a captain's bridge. This is where Mr. Aldrich held many meetings. The views of the ocean from this room are quite breathtaking. His heirs transferred some of the property to the Providence Diocese in 1939. By 1946, Our Lady of Providence Seminary was the new owner of the estate. They erected a campus and chapel for the school. When I was in high school we used to run major cross-country meets at the school. I never saw anything unusual but at the time I was not looking either. The school is gone now and the mansion has been reverted to its former state where functions are held regularly.

Although the family was very wealthy, it seems that not all his children were happy. Of his eight children, one of them reportedly committed suicide by jumping off of one of the balconies. Employees repeatedly encounter the restless spirit as they go about their daily duties. There is no reported place in particular the ghost seems to favor. She also appears and disappears whenever it is convenient to her. Being brought up in the house it would seem logical that she would materialize anywhere she wanted. Alarmed patrons of the facility have enquired about the ghost as well but it seems she mostly appears to the many employees that grace the manor for all the functions it serves.

The Aldrich's boathouse sits on the shore of the Narragansett Bay where it can be seen from Rocky Point Park as well. My grandmother once told me that my grandfather used to buy moonshine from the boathouse during prohibition. The boats would come in and signal, then unload the liquor. He would have a code used by the headlights of his automobile to indicate that he was a safe customer. Whether this was actually true or not I do not know but it makes a great story for the mansion none-the-less.

The mansion is located on the site of the former Our Lady of Providence Seminary. Take Interstate Route 95 to Route 117 East. Follow Route 117 to Warwick Neck Road. Take Warwick Neck Road to Aldrich Avenue. Bear left onto Aldrich Avenue and the old school and estate are on the right overlooking the water.

# West Greenwich

## "I AM WAITING AND WATCHING FOR YOU"

That is the inscription on the gravestone in Historical Cemetery No. 2 at the junctions of Plain Meeting House Road, Plain Road, and Liberty Hill Road in West Greenwich, Rhode Island. The cemetery is also marked by a small white meetinghouse (church) from which the road derives its name. Many strange occurrences have plagued this historical sight, but the most intriguing of all is the grave from which the above quote was taken.

Nellie Vaughn of Coventry died on March 1, 1889, at the age of nineteen from what might have been pneumonia. She originally was buried on the Vaughn farm in the family plot but later relocated to where she now

Spot where Nellie Vaughn was buried. Note that the ground looks rather barren for late summer.

rests, or at least lies. Maybe moving her from her original resting place set off the creepy chain of events that unfolded over time. A few people in the paranormal realm have told me she was buried alive by accident but I never read evidence to prove that theory. Either way, her plot is the only sunken grave in the burial ground and mysteriously continues to sink into the bowels of the earth. Another curious fact is that no flowers or other species of floriculture will grow upon the tomb. The barren domain of her resting place is easy to spot once within the stone walls of the burial ground.

She is said to be among the many undead that once roamed New England's countryside in search of the very blood they had lost in life. Reports of vampires in the eighteenth and nineteenth centuries gave birth to many a legend in New England. Among the New England states, Rhode Island was the most famous of all for vampirism. However, in Nellie's case, this accusation holds no validity according to historic records. She is also reported by many to still roam the sacred soil where she is buried. The latter statement does hold validity, according to various visitors to the cemetery over the years.

The most common occurrence has been a disembodied voice of a female echoing from around her grave. Many people have spotted a young woman walking around the cemetery in a white shroud. Most of the time she disappears when they come close. Some reports say she has actually spoken to a few individuals, then would be gone in the blink of an eye. Curious folk looking for grave rubbings of the infamous epitaph have come up short-handed for the stone will not transfer its inscription onto paper, no matter how hard one tries. I have a collection of rubbings from many of the stories I have written or witnessed stretching back many years. One piece of wall stands void of what should have been the homage to Nellie Vaughn.

Neither I nor anyone else I know has a copy of the marker in their possession. To make matters worse, the next time I visited the graveyard, the stone was gone. It has been taken and stored somewhere for safe keeping by the town. You can still find the plot just inside the wall, however, by the barren soil. Perhaps you might even see her hovering about "waiting and watching for you ..."

Nellie Vaughn's tomb is not the only landmark on the premises that has a peculiar allegation. The white meetinghouse still swells with the preaching of a long gone epoch when God-fearing settlers strode the byways to be cleansed by the word of the Lord. The little white church has supposedly sat silent by the cemetery stones for over one hundred years, but has it?

A friend related this account to me when he found out I knew of the place. He is a person of very few words and all are intelligently literal so when he has a tale to tell, you can bet that it is true. As he and his friends explored the grand piece of history, the bell on the church began to ring. Thinking it was one of his comrades playing a prank, he meandered around the other side of the building to scare the jokester. He then became completely startled when he rounded the church only to see the bell ringing by itself with no human hand to guide it. What became more startling was the fact that after the bell had ceased its tolling and they went to investigate, they found that the bell had no rope and more oddly, no *ringer*!

Plain meetinghouse overlooking Historical Cemetery #2, where accounts tell of ghostly sermons taking place behind the sealed doors.

A cousin (name withheld by request) was doing some genealogy on the family name as some of them are buried in this park of still tablets when he encountered a strange phenomenon. While he was logging information about the gravestones he heard voices coming from inside the meetinghouse. It appeared to be a sermon being preached in what sounded like "Old English" as he put it. When he went to the door and rapped on it, the voices floated out of existence and all was silent. He couldn't help but notice the door was padlocked from the outside and all the windows were boarded and padlocked as well. It was then he became a believer of the odd and unexplainable.

Next time you are in West Greenwich, Rhode Island, take a ride about three miles down Plain Meeting House Road to the old church itself. You might just get an earful.

Take Interstate Route 95 to Exit 5, Route 102 North. Take a left onto Plain Meeting House Road. The church is about four miles up at the junction. Please give the cemetery all the respect due under the law.

## Sharpe Street

Directly across from Plain Meeting House Road is another small rural paved way where another ghost is said to roam in the dead of night. Silas James was a gambler who met his match and fate one night over a game of cards. Accusations of cheating flew around the room followed by a broadax. Silas had murdered another gambler in cold blood. A trial ensued and poor Silas was hung for his crime in 1868. Now he is seen walking along the dark winding lane in the witching hours with his head hanging to one side from the noose pulling on it reciting the words that are written on his tombstone.

He is buried in the family's private burial ground and the words on his stone read, "Leave Judgment to Heaven." If you happen to be traversing that byway at night and see Silas, do yourself a favor and leave judgment to common sense and head the other way.

Follow directions for previous location, but take a right at Sharpe Street.

# West Warwick
## St. Mary's Church

Much legend abounds around this old church and accompanying burial ground. It is allegedly the oldest Catholic Church in Rhode Island. There is even a sign in front of the building that says so. Some scholars counter that claim by stating that the Newport Catholic Church is actually the oldest house of worship for that denomination in the state.

The fact is that the Protestants were here before the Catholics and did not care for their kind in the territory. When the plans for West Warwick's first Catholic church were completed, the Protestant people put a curse on the land saying that the first man to break ground will die a horrible death and be forever doomed to that spot.

The builder and clergy had a plan that would make a mockery of that curse. They had the builder's wife, Mary, shovel out the first chunk of earth. Since the curse said a "man" they figured all was safe. Unfortunately Mary passed away shortly after and, true to the curse, is forever fated to haunt the church. The clergy are aware of her but find no threat in her doings as she blows out candles and moves items to other locations of the church. She even likes to play with the lights. They have come to accept her presence as a normal occurrence while they go about their daily routines.

The cemetery belonging to the church is claimed to hold many spirits as well. Orbs have been photographed in the graveyard and EVP (Electronic Voice Phenomena) recordings have been taken in the place as well. Paranormal groups seem to love this plot of land for its ripe pickings in the spirit world. The interment records for the cemetery start in 1851. The name of the first interment on record is Mary Dalton. Make what you want of it.

The church is located at 70 Church Street. Take Interstate Route 95 to Exit 8, Route 2 North. Take Route 117 West. Take a left onto Main Street and that becomes Church Street after crossing Route 3.

# The Newsy Ghost of the
# Kent County Times Building

Some places seem like strange places for a ghost to reside, but when you think about it, a newspaper building is not so strange for spirit activity, especially when someone supposedly once committed suicide within its walls. Allegedly, a man once hung himself in the third floor stairwell of the building. Employees hear ghostly footsteps on the stairs and get the feeling they are being followed when using that staircase. It is said that the lavatory and storage rooms are haunted as well. When individuals enter the room, there is a gloomy haze in the air and a great feeling of dread overtakes them. The company of the spirit seems to follow many of the employees, watching their every move. Some people have quit out of fright from the presence of the ghost in the building. It could be the imaginations of those alone in a big old building or they really could have a newsy ghost on their hands. Story at midnight.

Follow previous directions. The building is at 1353 Main Street before the intersection of Route 3.

# Westerly

## Babcock-Smith House

When Joshua Babcock came to settle in Westerly, he had already made quite a name for himself. Not only was he a good friend of Benjamin Franklin, but he was a highly respected physician and active in politics as well. He built his two and one half story home in 1732 and there he lived up until his death in 1783. At one point, the house was used as the first post office in Westerly with Dr. Babcock as postmaster.

By 1812, his second wife had died and left the home to Dudley Babcock. He had to sell the estate to a distant relative, Oliver Wells, in 1817 to pay for the losses of his ships in the War of 1812. Wells turned it into a thriving tenant farm but also saw the mansion fall into heavy disrepair. In 1846 a stonemason by the name of Orlando Smith bought the estate after finding granite on the property. He paid eight thousand dollars for the property.

During that time, the Smith's turned the property into one of the finest and best known granite quarries in the world. With the advent of the Civil War, areas were made to hide slaves following the Underground Railroad. The tunnels in the basement that served as Indian escape routes in the early days were now used to hide the slaves. Over time the land was sold and is now in the hands of the Westerly Historical Commission. Many of its former residents still linger within the walls of the home for one reason or another.

Caretakers over the years have heard the voices of slaves in the five foot high tunnels where hundreds of slaves were crammed together on their leg of independence. There is no doubt a number of them died due to the appalling conditions in which they were forced to endure along their journey to Canada. One caretaker heard the phantom voice of a young slave coming from the closed tunnels. Though alarmed by the ghostly speech, he carefully jotted down what he could remember of the spectral conversation. He then went to the local library to check out the accounts he had overheard and was flabbergasted as he read the historical recollections of one slave who had related his journey to the house. It was the same story he had heard from the phantom voice in the tunnels.

The Babcock-Smith House is located at 124 Granite Street. Take Interstate Route 95 to Exit 1, Route 3 South. Follow to Route 1 and take a left turn onto Granite Street where Route 3 and Route 1 intersect.

# Napatree Point

If any place deserves to be haunted, it would be Napatree Point. Not only was it a fort during World War I, the community was washed out to sea during the 1938 hurricane. The community was once part on Watch Hill Harbor. It was built on a sandbar at the southern tip of Rhode Island. A narrow road ran from the mainland through the point to the ruins of the old fort. The people of the harbor led normal lives. The children would play among the ruins of the old army fort and the world seemed right. Then came the hurricane of 1938. It was a devastating storm that ravaged most of Rhode Island. Watch Hill never had a chance. The homes along the sandbar were torn from their foundations and dragged out to sea. Many people perished in the tragedy. Even the sturdy fortress was demolished and parts of it sent to a watery grave. Years after the storm, artifacts from the houses still wash up on shore. So many objects have been found on the point that the people of Watch Hill have dubbed that area "The Kitchen." Divers take delight in searching for small trinkets scattered about the ocean floor. Unfortunately, those who once owned them are still looking for their possessions and loved ones.

When the sands are void of walkers and adventurers, voices of the past are still heard reliving those frightful moments that sealed the fate of the little village. The wind carries them along the shores and up the hill where unsuspecting lovers might be holding hands ... or a local resident is walking a dog. The horrific, unearthly cries are enough to make the hair on the back of your neck stand up.

Some remains of the fort still protrude from portions of the sand dunes. Here and there you will find a portal to the old garrison. This only adds to the uncanny atmosphere surrounding Napatree Point. The old timers will tell you about the hurricane of 1938. It was brutal. It has left an indelible mark on the area. A mark that still echoes in the wind.

Napatree Point is the southwestern tip of Rhode Island. Take Interstate Route 95 to Exit 1, Route 3 South. Take Route 1A to Watch Hill Road. Follow Watch Hill Road to Westerly Road and Bluff Avenue. Take a right onto Larkin Road and then a left onto Fortress Road. There you will see a parking lot. Follow the path for one and one half miles to the point.

# Woonsocket
## Precious Blood Cemetery

Woonsocket is a very small city. That doesn't mean it can't have a ghost or two floating around. Many residents claim they live in a haunted house. No one wants people poking around and invading their privacy while looking for ghosts. I can't say I blame them. There is one place where the public is welcome and even paranormal groups like to visit. That is the Precious Blood Cemetery.

The atmosphere of this burial ground is very creepy, even on the brightest days. Various paranormal groups have been drawn to this cemetery for investigations. The results are usually the same. People have photographed orbs hovering over the graves. Local residents claim to have seen shadowy figures walking among the gravestones. A few people claim to have recorded EVP voices on tape. There are sixteen thousand burials in the cemetery, making it by far the largest burial ground in Woonsocket. It's no wonder there are so many reports of ghosts and balls of energy in this place. The investigations are ongoing in this cemetery, but everyone who visits leaves with the same conclusion we did. There is definitely something supernatural going on inside those gates.

Precious Blood Cemetery is located at the corners of Diamond Hill Road and Rathbun Street. Take Interstate 295 to Exit 11, Route 114 West. Follow into Woonsocket and the cemetery is just past intersection of Route 126.

# Bibliography

Bell, Michael E. *Food for the Dead*. New York, New York: Carroll and Graf Publishers, 2001.

Boisvert, Donald J. *Rhode Island Vampires, Eerie Spirits, and Ghostly Apparitions*. North Kingstown, Rhode Island: Old Rhode Island, 1992.

Cahill, Robert Ellis. *Lighthouse Mysteries of the North Atlantic*. Salem, Massachusetts: Old Saltbox Publishing, 1998.

Guiley, Rosemary Ellen. *The Encyclopedia of Ghosts and Spirits*. New York, New York: Checkmark Books, 2000.

Jasper, Mark. *Haunted Inns of New England*. Yarmouth Port, Massachusetts: On Cape Publications, 2000.

Kennedy, Dennis. *Haunted by Local Legends*. Smithfield, Rhode Island: Observer Publications, 1992.

Pitkin, David J. *Ghosts of the Northeast*. Salem, New York: Aurora Publications, 2002.

Robinson, Charles Turek. *The New England Ghost Files*. North Attleborough, Massachusetts: Covered Bridge Press, 1994.

Scott, Michael Norman and Beth. *Historic Haunted America*. New York, New York: Tom Doherty Associates, LLC, 1995.

Smitten, Susan. *Ghost Stories of New England*. Auburn, Washington: Lone Pine Publishing, 2003.

# Index